Roadtrippers Guide to the United States

Volume 1

Washington, Oregon, Idaho, Montana, Wyoming, North Dakota, South Dakota

Madison Gabrielle

Fulton Books
Meadville, PA

Published by Fulton Books 2022

ISBN 978-1-63710-725-6 (paperback)
ISBN 978-1-63985-439-4 (hardcover)
ISBN 978-1-63710-726-3 (digital)

Printed in the United States of America

To John Paul Wheaton, the Wheaton family, and his faithful furry travel companion, Spud.

Introduction

Have you ever dreamed of road-tripping across the country? Are you interested in seeing unknown gems dotted across these great states? If so, *Roadtrippers Guide to the United States* is your go-to guide that will get you to these places with ease. Each location featured in this book has everything you'll need for a road trip of a lifetime. I've done years of exploring, researching, and traveling to make sure this book helps you get to where *you didn't even know you needed to go to,* all without you lifting a finger for research. I offer you all of this great information so you can get to your destination easily, including

- detailed directions from the largest major city,
- entrance fees,
- hours of operation,
- applicable phone numbers, and much more.

In this book, there is a roadside attraction for everyone: caves, waterfalls, native sites, historical locations, obscure roadside stops, and everything in between. Please be respectful of all of the sites you visit and follow local rules and guidelines. Most importantly, don't forget to enjoy yourself and take time to savor moments of your journey…because that's what this book is all about!

Truly,
Madison Gabrielle
Fellow wanderlust explorer

Washington

Museum of Glass (obscure)
1801 Dock Street, Tacoma, Washington 98402
(253)284-4750
Call for museum hours
$17
From Seattle, head south on I-5 toward Tacoma. In 30.0 miles, take exit 133 onto SR-7 south toward City Center. In 600 feet, keep right onto East 26th Street. In 350 feet, keep right onto East 26th Street. In 0.3 miles, turn right onto East 26th Street. In 600 feet, turn left onto East D Street. In 0.2 miles, turn left onto Dock Street. In 0.4 miles, your destination will be on your right.

The Fremont Troll (obscure)
3405 Troll Avenue North, Seattle, Washington 98103
(206)547-7440
Free
Open 24 hours
From Tacoma, head north on I-5 toward Seattle. In 33.0 miles, take exit 167 onto Mercer Street toward Seattle Center. In 0.6 miles, continue onto Mercer Street. In 0.4 miles, turn right onto Dexter Avenue North. In 350 feet, turn left onto Roy Street. In 300 feet, turn right onto Aurora Avenue North. In 1.8 miles, take a slight right turn onto Bridge Way North. In 600 feet, take a slight right turn onto North 38th Street. In 250 feet, turn right onto Albion Place North. In 800 feet, turn right onto North 36th Street. In 700 feet, your destination will be on your right.

Museum of Pop Culture (obscure)
325 5th Avenue N, Seattle, Washington 98109
(206)770-2700
Friday–Sunday 10:00 a.m.–6:00 p.m.
$28
From Tacoma, head north on I-5 toward Seattle. In 33.0 miles, take exit 167 to merge onto Mercer Street toward Seattle Center. In 0.6 miles, continue onto Mercer Street. In 0.6 miles, turn left onto 5th Avenue North. In 900 feet, your destination will be on your right.

Olympic Sculpture Park (obscure)
2901 Western Avenue., Seattle, Washington 98121
(206)654-3100
6:00 a.m.–5:00 p.m.
$22
From Tacoma, head north on I-5 toward Seattle. In 32.0 miles, take exit 165 toward Seneca Street. In 0.2 miles, continue onto Seneca Street. In 0.3 miles, turn right onto 1st Avenue. In 1.0 mile, turn left onto Broad Street. In 600 feet, turn right onto Elliot Avenue. In 350 feet, your destination will be on your left.

The Museum of Flight (obscure)
9404 E Marginal Way S, Seattle, Washington 98108
(206)764-5700
Thursday–Sunday 10:00 a m.–5:00 p.m.
$25

From Tacoma, head north on I-5 toward Seattle. In 22.0 miles, take a slight right turn to merge onto SR-599 north toward Tukwila. In 1.8 miles, take exit onto Tukwila Intl Boulevard north. In 300 feet, continue onto East Marginal Way South. In 0.7 miles, turn right onto Museum of Flight Place South. In 400 feet, turn left into the parking lot. You have arrived at your destination.

Pacific Science Center (obscure)

200 2nd Avenue, N, Seattle, Washington 98109

(206)443-2001

Wednesday–Friday 10:00 a.m.–5:00 p.m.; Saturday–Sunday 10:00 a.m.–6:00 p.m.

$23.95

From Tacoma, head north on I-5 toward Seattle. In 32.0 miles, take exit 165 toward Seneca Street. In 0.4 miles, turn right onto 4th Avenue. In 1.0 mile, turn left onto West Denny Way. In 500 feet, take a slight right turn. You have arrived at your destination.

The Teapot Dome Gas Station (obscure)

117 1st Avenue, Zillah, Washington 98953

(509)829-5100

24/7

Free to look

From Kennewick, head west on SR-240. In 6.4 miles, keep right on SR-240, west toward I-182, west toward Yakima. In 1.2 miles, continue onto I-182 West. In 4.0 miles, take exit onto I-82 west toward Yakima. In 50.0 miles, take exit 52 toward Toppenish. In 0.3 miles, turn right onto West First Avenue toward Zillah. In 0.4 miles, your destination will be on your left.

Space Needle (obscure)

400 Broad Street, Seattle, Washington 98109

(206)905-2100

Monday–Thursday 12:00 p.m.–5:00 p.m.; Friday 12:00 p.m.–6:00 p.m.; Saturday–Sunday 11:00 a.m.–5:00 p.m.

$24.50–$37.50

From Tacoma, head north on I-5 toward Seattle. In 36.0 miles, take exit 167 onto Mercer Street toward Seattle Center. In 0.6 miles, continue onto Mercer Street. In 0.6 miles, turn left onto 5th Avenue north. In 0.3 miles, take a slight right turn onto Broad Street. In 450 feet, turn right. In 200 feet, your destination will be on your right.

Grand Coulee Dam Laser Show (obscure)

17 Midway Avenue, Grand Coulee, Washington 99133
(509)633-3074
Free show
Memorial Day–September 30
From Spokane, head west on I-90. In 2.3 miles, take exit 277 onto US-2 west toward Davenport. In 600 feet, stay left onto US-2 west toward Davenport. In 3.8 miles, at the roundabout, take the second exit onto West Sunset Highway. In 2.8 miles, at the roundabout, take the first exit onto West Sunset Highway. In 56.0 miles, turn right onto SR-21. In 0.5 miles onto SR-174. In 19.0 miles, turn right onto Spokane Way. In 0.3 miles, stay right onto Federal Avenue. In 0.3 miles, turn right onto SR-155. In 1.7 miles, your destination will be on your right.

Seattle Underground (obscure)

614 1st Avenue, Seattle, WA 98104
(206)682-4646
Sunday–Wednesday 9:30 a.m.–6:00 p.m.; Thursday–Saturday 9:30 a.m.–8:00 p.m.
Adult $22, Youths $10
From Tacoma, head north on I-5 toward Seattle. In 31.0 miles, take exit 164B onto East Martinez Drive. In 0.7 miles, turn right onto Edgar Martinez Drive South. In 0.2 miles, turn right onto 1st Avenue South. In 0.8 miles, continue onto 1st Avenue. In 250 feet, destination will be on your right.

Seattle Metaphysical Library (obscure)

2220 NW Market Street, Seattle, Washington 98107
(206)329-1794
Sunday 2:00 p.m.–6:00 p.m.
Free to look
From Tacoma, head north on I-5 toward Seattle. In 33.0 miles, take exit 167 onto Mercer Street. In 0.6 miles, continue onto Mercer Street. In 0.2 miles, turn right onto Westlake Avenue North. In 900 feet, turn right onto 9th Avenue North. In 2.8 miles, keep left onto West Nickerson Street. In 700 feet, take a slight right turn toward Ballard Bridge. In 300 feet, continue onto 15th Avenue West. In 0.5 miles, take a slight right turn toward Canal Locks. In 700 feet, turn left onto NW Leary Way. In 0.5 miles, turn left onto NW Market Street. In 300 feet, your destination will be on your right.

Pike Place Market (obscure)
85 Pike Street, Seattle, Washington 98101
(206)682-7453
7:00 a.m.–11:00 p.m.
Free
From Tacoma, head north on I-5 toward Seattle. In 32.0 miles, take exit 165 toward Seneca Street. In 0.2 miles, turn right onto 6th Avenue. In 700 feet, turn left onto Union Street. In 0.2 miles, your destination will be on your right.

Greenwood Space Travel Supply (obscure)
8414 Greenwood Avenue North, Seattle, Washington 98103
(206)725-2625
Tuesday 11:00 a.m.–5:00 p.m.; Thursday 11:00 a.m.–2:00 p.m.
Free to look
From Tacoma, head north on I-5 toward Seattle. In 37.0 miles, take exit 172 onto N 85th Street toward Aurora Avenue North. In 1.6 miles, turn left onto Greenwood Avenue. In 100 feet, your destination is on your left.

Chihuly Garden and Glass (obscure)
305 Harrison Street, Seattle, Washington 98109
(206)753-4940
Daily 12:00 p.m.–5:00 p.m.
$32
From Tacoma, head north on I-5 toward Seattle. In 33.0 miles, take exit 167 onto Mercer Street toward Seattle Center. In 0.6 miles, turn left onto 5th Avenue North. In 0.3 miles, take a slight right turn onto Broad Street. In 450 feet, turn right. In 300 feet, prepare to park your vehicle. Your destination will be on your right.

Ye Olde Curiosity Shop (obscure)
1001 Alaskan Way Pier 54, Seattle, Washington 98104
(206)682-5844
Sunday–Thursday 11:00 a.m.–6:00 p.m.; Friday–Saturday 10:00 a.m.–8:00 p.m.
Free to look
From Tacoma, head north on I-5 toward Seattle. In 30.0 miles, take exit 164A toward Madison Street. In 800 feet, keep left onto Dearborn Street toward Madison Street. In 0.3 miles, keep left onto 7th Avenue. In 0.7 miles, keep right toward Madison Street. In 0.3 miles, turn left onto Madison Street. In 0.5 miles, turn right onto Alaskan Way. In 200 feet, your destination will be on your left.

Maryhill Museum of Art/Stonehenge (obscure)
35 Maryhill Museum Drive, Goldendale, Washington 98620
(509)773-3733
Adults $12, Youths $5
10:00 a.m.–5:00 p.m.
From Kennewick, head west on US-395. In 4.0 miles, continue onto I-82 East. In 29.0 miles, keep right on I-84 West toward Portland. In 75.0 miles, take exit 104 onto US-97 toward Yakima. In 0.2 miles, turn right onto US-97 toward Goldendale. In 2.4 miles, turn right onto SR-14. In 1.0 mile, turn right onto Stonehenge Drive. In 0.7 miles, your destination will be on your right.

Port Angeles Underground (obscure)

121 Railroad Avenue, Port Angeles, Washington 98362

(360)460-5748

Winter and spring 2:00 p.m.; summer and fall 10:00 a.m. and 2:00 p.m. Monday–Saturday

Adults $15, Youths $8

From Tacoma, head south on I-5 toward Portland. In 22.0 miles, take exit 132B to merge onto SR-16. In 0.5 miles, keep left to merge onto SR-16 West. In 26.0 miles, continue onto West State Highway 16. In 0.9 miles, merge onto SR-3 North. In 1.9 miles, keep left onto SR-3 North toward Silverdale. In 17.0 miles, continue onto State Highway 3 NW. In 6.3 miles, turn left onto Hood Canal Floating Bridge. In 15.0 miles, make a slight right onto SR-104 West. In 0.3 miles, continue onto US-101. Stay on the 101 for 28.0 miles. In 7.0 miles, take a slight right onto East Front Street. In 1.6 miles, turn right onto North Lincoln Street. In 350 feet, turn left onto East Railroad Avenue. In 150 feet, your destination will be on your right.

Spark Museum of Electrical Invention (obscure)

1312 Bay Street, Bellingham, Washington 98225

(360)738-3886

Wednesday–Sunday 11:00 a.m.–5:00 p.m.

$6

From Seattle, head north on I-5 toward Vancouver, B.C. In 88.0 miles, take exit 253 toward Lakeway Drive. In 0.9 miles, turn right onto Bay Street. In 90 feet, keep right onto Bay Street. Your destination will be on your right.

The Hobbit House at Brothers Greenhouse and Nursery (obscure)

3200 Victory Drive SW, Port Orchard, Washington 98367

(360)674-2558

9:00 a.m.–3:00 p.m.

Free to look

From Tacoma, head south on I-5 toward Portland. In 1.2 miles, take exit 132B to merge onto SR-16. In 0.5 miles, keep left to merge onto SR-16 West. In 26.0 miles, continue onto West SH-16. In 0.5 miles, take exit 28 onto SR-3 South toward Belfair. In 0.5 miles, turn left onto SR-3. In 1.7 miles, turn left onto Sunnyslope Road SW. In 200 feet, turn left onto Victory Drive SW. In 500 feet, take a slight right turn. You have arrived at your destination.

Blue Fox Drive-In Movie Theater (obscure; ferry required)
1403 North Monroe Landing Road, Oak Harbor, Washington 98277
(360)675-5667
$10
Movie time may vary
From Seattle, head north on I-5 north toward Vancouver, British Colombia. In 64.0 miles, take exit 230 onto SR-20 toward Burlington. In 0.4 miles, turn left onto SR-20 toward San Juan. In 12.0 miles, at the roundabout, take the second exit onto SR-20. In 0.6 miles, at the roundabout, take the second exit onto SR-20. In 8.0 miles, at the roundabout, take the second exit onto SR-20. In 7.8 miles, turn right onto SR-20. In 2.1 miles, turn left onto North Monroes Landing Road. In 0.2 miles, turn right. In 100 feet, your destination will be on your left.

Seattle Art Museum (obscure)
1300 1st Avenue, Seattle, Washington 98101
(206)654-3100
Thursday 10:00 a.m.–9:00 p.m.; Friday–Sunday, Wednesday 10:00 a.m.–5:00 p.m.
$12+
From Tacoma, head north on I-5 toward Seattle. In 32.0 miles, take exit 165 toward Seneca Street. In 0.2 miles, turn right onto 6th Avenue. In 15 feet, turn left onto Seneca Street. In 0.3 miles, turn right onto 1st Avenue. In 500 feet, your destination will be on your right.

Ex Nihilo Sculpture Park (obscure)
22410 SR-706 E, Ashford, Washington 98330
Daily
Donation
From Seattle, head south on I-5 toward Portland. In 9.9 miles, take exit 154A to merge onto I-405 North toward Renton. In 2.0 miles, take exit 2 to merge onto SR-167 South toward Auburn. In 0.3 miles, keep right to merge onto SR-167 South toward Kent. In 20.0 miles, take a slight right turn to merge onto SR-161 South toward Puyallup. In 3.4 miles, take exit onto SR-161 South toward Eatonville. In 0.4 miles, turn left onto 31st Avenue SW toward Mt. Rainier, in 15.0 miles keep left onto Meridian Avenue East, in 8.3 miles turn left onto Center Street East. In 7.2 miles, turn left onto Mountain Highway East. In 4.9 miles, continue onto SR-706 East. In 2.8 miles, your destination will be on your right.

Camlann Medieval Village (obscure)

10320 Kelly Road, NE, Carnation, Washington 98014

(425)788-8624

Saturday and Sunday 12:00 p.m.–5:00 p.m.

Free to look

From Seattle, head east on I-90 toward Spoaken. In 20.0 miles, take exit 22 toward Preston. In 0.2 miles, turn left onto Preston-Fall City Road. In 900 feet, turn right onto SE High Point Way. In 4.4 miles, turn right onto Fall City Carnation Road SE. In 700 feet, at the roundabout, take the second exit onto Fall City Carnation Road SE. In 8.8 miles, turn right onto NE Stillwater Hill Road. In 1.1 miles, turn right into parking lot. You have arrived at your destination.

John S. McMillin Memorial Mausoleum (obscure; ferry required)

664 Afterglow Drive, Friday Harbor, Washington 98250

Sunrise to sunset

Free

From Seattle, head north on I-5. In 64.0 miles, take exit 230 onto SR-20 toward Burlington. In 0.4 miles, turn left onto SR-20 toward San Juan. In 12.0 miles, keep right onto SR-20 Spur. In 2.8 miles, at the roundabout, take the first exit onto Commercial Avenue. In 1.3 miles, turn left onto 12th Street. In 2.7 miles, at the roundabout, take the second exit onto Oakes Avenue. In 0.4 miles, keep right onto Ferry Terminal Road. In 0.7 miles, take the Washington State ferry. In 19.0 miles, continue ahead. In 300 feet, turn right onto Front Street South. In 300 feet, take a sharp left turn onto Spring Street. In 40 feet, turn right onto Spring Street. In 500 feet, turn right onto Second Street South. In 0.3 miles, turn right onto Tucker Avenue. In 0.4 miles, keep left onto Roche Harbor Road. In 8.6 miles, take a slight right turn onto Afterglow Drive. In 0.2 miles, your destination will be on your right.

Dandelion Botanical Company Herbal Shop (obscure)
4681 Sequim-Dungeness Way, Sequim, Washington 98382
(206)545-8892
Monday–Saturday 10:00 a.m.–5:00 p.m.
Free to look
From Tacoma, head south on I-5. In 1.2 miles, take exit 132B to merge onto SR-16. In 0.5 miles, keep left to merge onto SR-16 West. In 26.0 miles, continue onto West SH-16 West. In 0.9 miles, merge onto SR-3 North. In 1.9 miles, keep left on SR-3 North toward Silverdale. In 17.0 miles, continue onto SH-3 NW. In 6.3 miles, turn left onto Hood Canal Floating Bridge. In 15.0 miles, keep right onto SR-104 West. In 0.3 miles, continue onto US-101. In 20.0 miles, keep right onto Sequim Avenue toward City Center. In 0.3 miles, turn right onto South Sequim Avenue. In 1.4 miles, at the roundabout, take the second exit onto Sequim-Dungeness Way. In 3.6 miles, turn right onto Sequim-Dungeness Way. In 400 feet, your destination will be on your left.

Henry Art Gallery (obscure)
NE 41st Street and 15th Avenue NE, Seattle, Washington 98105
(206)543-2280
Wednesday, Friday–Sunday 11:00 a.m.–4:00 p.m.; Thursday 11:00 a.m.–9:00 p.m.
$10
From Tacoma, head north on I-5 toward Seattle. In 32.0 miles, keep left on I-5 North. In 3.7 miles, take exit onto NE 42nd Street. In 800 feet, continue onto NE 42nd Street. In 700 feet, turn right onto Roosevelt Way NE. In 500 feet, turn left onto NE Campus Parkway. In 0.3 miles, turn left onto 15th Avenue NE. In 100 feet, your destination will be on your right.

The Cheesemonger's Cheese Shop (obscure)
819 Front Street, Leavenworth, Washington 98826
(877)888-7389
Sunday–Thursday 10:00 a.m.–6:00 p.m.; Friday–Saturday 10:00 a.m.–8:00 p.m.
Free to look
From Seattle, head east on I-90 toward Spokane. In 6.9 miles, take exit 10A to merge onto I-405 North toward Everett. In 0.5 miles, keep left to merge onto I-405 North. In 12.0 miles, take exit 23 to merge onto SR-522 toward Woodinville. In 0.9 miles, keep right to merge onto SR-522 East. In 13.0 miles, keep right onto US-2 East toward Wenatchee. In 10.0 miles, at the round-about, take the second exit onto US-2 East. In 75.0 miles, turn right onto Front Street. In 800 feet, you will arrive at your destination.

Rubber Chicken Museum (obscure)

1300 N 45th Street, Seattle, Washington 98130

(206)297-0240

11:00 a.m.–5:00 p.m.

Free

From Tacoma, head north on I-5 toward Seattle. In 35.0 miles, take exit 169 onto NE 45th Street. I n 500 feet, keep right onto NE 45th Street. In 0.2 miles, turn left onto NE 45th Street. In 1.0 mile, your destination will be on your right.

Sanford & Sons Antiques and Auctions (obscure)

743 Broadway, Tacoma, Washington 98402

(253)272-0334

Wednesday–Saturday 11:00 a.m–5:00 p.m.; Sunday 12:00 p.m.–5:00 p.m.

Free to look

From Seattle, head south on I-5 toward Tacoma. In 30.0 miles, take exit 133 to merge onto I-705 North toward City Center. In 600 feet, keep left to merge onto I-705 North. In 350 feet, keep left onto I-705 North. In 0.7 miles, keep left toward A Street. In 0.3 miles, keep right onto A Street. In 0.3 miles, keep left onto A Street. In 0.3 miles, turn left onto South 9th Street. In 700 feet, turn right onto Broadway. In 400 feet, your destination will be on your right.

Palouse Falls (nature)

Palouse Falls, Lacrosse, Washington 99143

(509)646-9218

8:00 a.m.–5:10 p.m.

$10

From Seattle, head east on I-90 toward Spokane. In 108.0 miles, keep left on I-90 East. In 27.0 miles, take exit 137 onto SR-26 East toward Pullman. In 83.0 miles, turn right onto North Main Street. In 6.4 miles, turn left onto SR-261. In 8.7 miles, turn left onto Palouse Falls Road. In 2.3 miles, you will arrive at your destination.

Olympic Hot Springs (nature; hiking required)

Appleton Pass Trail, Port Angeles, WA 98363

Daily

Free

From Port Angeles, head west on US-101. In 8.3 miles, turn left onto Olympic Hot Springs Road. In 5.5 miles, take a sharp right turn onto Olympic Hot Springs Road. In 4.5 miles, prepare to park your vehicle near Boulder Hot Springs Trail. Continue onto Boulder Hot Springs Trail. In 2.4 miles, take a left onto Boulder Hot Springs Trail. In 670 feet, your destination will be on your right.

Ape Cave (nature; hiking required)
Forest Road 8303, Cougar, WA 98616
(360)891-5000
Daily
$5
From Tacoma, head south on I-5 toward Portland. In 111.0 miles, take exit 22 onto Dike Access Road. In 0.4 miles, at the roundabout, take the third exit onto Dike Access Road. In 600 feet, at the roundabout, take the first exit onto Old Pacific Highway. In 0.9 miles, take a slight left onto East Scott Avenue. In 0.2 miles, at the roundabout, take the second exit onto Lewis River Road. In 22.0 miles, continue onto Lewis River Road. In 12.0 miles, turn left. In 1.7 miles, turn left onto Forest Service Road 8303. In 0.9 miles, turn into parking lot. In 600 feet, you will arrive at your destination.

Madison Creek Falls (nature; hiking required)
1930 Olympic Hot Springs Road, Port Angeles, Washington 98363
6:00 a.m.–5:30 p.m.
Free
From Tacoma, head south on I-5 toward Portland. In 1.2 miles, take exit 132B to merge onto SR-16. In 0.5 miles, keep left to merge onto SR-16 West. In 26.0 miles, continue onto West SH-16. In 0.9 miles, merge onto SR-3 North. In 1.9 miles, keep left on SR-3 North toward Silverdale. In 17.0 miles, continue onto SH-3 NW. In 6.3 miles, turn left onto Hood Canal Floating Bridge. In 15.0 miles, keep right onto SR-104 West. In 0.3 miles, continue onto US-101. In 28.0 miles, keep left onto US-101. In 7.0 miles, take a slight right turn onto East Front Street. In 1.6 miles, continue onto East Front Street. In 0.7 miles, turn left on Tumwater Truck Route. In 1.5 miles, continue onto West Highway 101. In 6.5 miles, turn left onto Olympic Hot Springs Road. In 2.1 miles, prepare to park your vehicle, take a sharp left turn onto Madison Creek Falls Nature Trail. In 290 feet, you will arrive at your destination.

Wallaby Ranch (nature)
35303 SE Fish Hatchery Road, Fall City, Washington 98024
(206)354-8624
$15
Daily (call for appointment)
From Seattle, take I-90 east toward Bellevue. In 20.0 miles, take exit 22 toward Preston-Fall City. In 0.2 miles, turn left onto Preston-Fall City Road. In 900 feet, turn right onto SE High Point Way. In 4.4 miles, turn right onto Fall City Carnation Road SE. In 600 feet, take a slight right turn onto SE Fall City Snoqualmie Road. In 0.8 miles, turn right onto SE Fish Hatchery Road. In 0.2 miles, your destination will be on your right.

Hall of Mosses (nature; hiking required)
Hall of Mosses Nature Trail, Forks, Washington 98331
(360)565-2985
Open 24 hours
$30
From Tacoma, head South on I-5 toward Portland. In 29.0 miles, take exit 104 to merge onto US-101 North toward Aberdeen. In 5.8 miles, continue onto SR-8 West toward Montesano. In 20.0 miles, merge onto SR-8 West. In 1.1 miles, continue onto US-12 West. In 11.0 miles, take exit toward Devonshire Road. In 900 feet, continue onto Wynooche Valley Road. In 8.8 miles, turn left onto Wynoochee Wishkah Road. In 4.6 miles, turn right onto Wishkah Road. In 2.1 miles, turn left onto Hoquiam Wishkah Road. In 1.7 miles, turn right onto East Hoquiam Road. In 5.2 miles, turn right onto US-101. In 76.0 miles, turn right onto Upper Hoh Road. In 18.0 miles, turn right. In 900 feet, prepare to park your vehicle near Hoh Visitor Center Mini-Loop Nature Trail. Take a right onto Mini Loop Trail. In 370 feet, take a left onto Hall of Mosses Nature Trail. In 850 feet, you will arrive at your destination.

Second Beach (nature)
13370 La Push Road, Forks, Washington 98331
Daily
Free
From Tacoma, head south on I-5 toward Portland. In 29.0 miles, take exit 104 to merge onto US-101 North toward Aberdeen. In 5.9 miles, continue onto SR-8 West toward Montesano. In 20.0 miles, merge onto SR-8 West. In 1.1 miles, continue onto US-12 West. In 11.0 miles, take exit toward Devonshire Road. In 900 feet, continue onto Wynoochee Valley Road. In 8.8 miles, turn left onto Wynoochee Wishkah Road. In 4.6 miles, turn right onto Wishkah Road. In 2.1 miles, turn left onto Hoquiam Wishkah Road. In 1.7 miles, turn right onto East Hoquiam Road. In 5.2 miles, turn right onto US-101. In 91.0 miles, turn left onto La Push Road. In 13.0 miles, your destination will be on your left.

One Square Inch of Silence (Nature; hiking required)
Olympic National Park, Hoh River Trail, Forks, Washington 98331
Free
Daily
From Tacoma, head south on I-5 toward Portland. In 29.0 miles, take exit 104 to merge onto US-101 North toward Aberdeen. Continue onto SR-8 West toward Montesano. In 21.0 miles, continue onto US-12 West. In 11.0 miles, take exit toward Devonshire Road. In 900 feet, continue onto Wynooche Valley Road. In 8.8 miles, turn left onto Wynoochee Wishkah Road. In 4.6 miles, turn right onto Wishkah Road. In 2.1 miles, turn left onto Hoquiam Wishkah Road. In 1.7 miles, turn right onto Hoquiam Road. In 5.2 miles, turn right onto US-101. In 76.0 miles, turn right onto Upper Hoh Road. In 18.0 miles, turn right. In 900 feet, prepare to park your car near the Hoh Visitor Center. Once you have arrived at the Hoh Rain Forest Visitor Center, head right onto Hoh Visitor Center Mini Loop Nature Trail. In 80 feet, take a right onto Hoh Visitor Center Mini Loop Trail. In 330 feet, take a right onto Spruce Bottom Nature Trail. In 100 feet, take a slight left turn onto Hoh River Trail. In 3.3 miles, your destination will be on your left.

Ruby Beach (nature)
Forks, Washington 98331
(360)565-3130
Daily
$15
From Port Angeles, head west on US-101. In 83.0 miles, turn right onto Ruby Beach Road. In 150 feet, prepare to park your vehicle near Ruby Beach Road.

Elandan Gardens (nature)
3050 WA-16, Bremerton, Washington 98312
(360)373-8260
Tuesday–Sunday 10:00 a.m.–4:00 p.m.
$6.50
From Tacoma, head south on I-5 toward Portland. In 1.2 miles, take exit 132B to merge onto SR-16. In 0.5 miles, merge onto SR-16 West. In 26.0 miles, continue onto West State Highway 16. In 700 feet, your destination is on your right.

Deception Falls (nature)
Stevens Pass Hwy, Skykomish, Washington 98288
Daily
Free
From Seattle, head east on I-90 toward Spokane. In 6.9 miles, take exit 10A to merge onto I-405 North toward Everett. In 0.5 miles, stay left to merge onto I-405 North. In 12.0 miles, take exit 23 to merge onto SR-522 toward Woodinville. In 0.9 miles, keep right to merge onto SR-522 East. In 13.0 miles, keep right onto US-2 East toward Wenatchee. In 10.0 miles, at the roundabout, take the second exit onto US-2 East. In 33.0 miles, prepare to park your vehicle near Deception Falls. Take a left onto Deception Falls Trail. In 670 feet, you will arrive at your destination.

Twin Sisters (nature; hiking required)
Touchet, Washington 99360
Daily
Free
From Spokane, head west on I-90. In 59.0 miles, take exit 220 to merge onto US-395 South toward Ritzville. In 74.0 miles, take a slight right turn to merge onto US-12 East toward Walla Walla. In 0.3 miles, keep left to merge onto US-12 East. In 17.0 miles, keep right onto US-730 West. In 2.1 miles, your destination will be on your left.

Olympic National Park (nature) (ferry required)
3002 Mount Angeles Road, Port Angeles, Washington 98362
(360)565-3130
24-7
$30
From Seattle, head north on I-5 toward Vancouver, B.C. In 12.0 miles, take exit 177 onto SR-104 toward Edmonds. In 700 feet, keep left onto SR-104 West. In 0.3 miles, keep right onto SR-104 West toward Kingston Ferry. In 0.2 miles, turn right onto Lake Ballinger Way. In 1.0 mile, keep right onto Edmonds Way. In 2.4 miles, take a slight right turn onto Edmonds Way. In 1.3 miles, turn left onto Main Street. In 0.2 miles, take the Washington State ferry. In 5.6 miles, continue ahead. In 4.1 miles, turn right onto SH-104 NE. In 5.0 miles, turn right onto Hood Canal Floating Bridge. In 15.0 miles, keep right onto SR-104 West. In 0.3 miles, continue onto US101. In 7.0 miles, take a slight right turn onto East Front Street. In 0.9 miles, turn left onto North Race Street. In 1.1 miles, turn right into the parking lot. You have arrived at your destination.

Discovery Park (nature)
3801 Discovery Park Boulevard, Seattle, Washington 98199
(206)684-4075
4:00 a.m.–9:30 p.m.
$15.95
From Tacoma, head north on I-5 toward Seattle. In 33.0 miles, take exit 167 onto Mercer Street toward Seattle Center. In 0.6 miles, continue onto Mercer Street. In 0.2 miles, turn right onto Westlake Avenue North. In 900 feet, turn right onto 9th Avenue North. In 2.8 miles, keep left onto West Nickerson Street. In 900 feet, turn left onto West Emerson Street. In 0.2 miles, turn left onto West Emerson Street. In 0.3 miles, turn right onto 21st Avenue West. In 1.6 miles, turn left onto 40th Avenue West. In 600 feet, turn right onto Texas Way West. In 500 feet, take a slight right turn into the parking lot. You have arrived at your destination.

Cape Flattery (nature; hiking required)
Cape Loop Road, Sekiu, Washington 98381
24-7
Free
From Port Angeles, head West on US-101. In 44.0 miles, turn right onto Burnt Mountain Road. In 10.0 miles, continue onto SR-112. In 27.0 miles, turn left on Fort Street. In 500 feet, turn right onto Third Avenue. In 350 feet, turn left onto Cape Flattery Road. In 7.6 miles, your destination will be on your right.

Dry Falls (nature)
Coulee City, Washington 99115
(509)632-5214
Daily
Free
From Seattle, head East on I-90 toward Spokane. In 108.0 miles, keep left on I-90 East toward Spokane. In 41.0 miles, take exit 151 toward SR-283 North toward Ephrata. In 0.6 miles, turn right onto SR-283 North. In 15.0 miles, continue onto Highway 28 West. In 11.0 miles, turn left onto SR-17. In 19.0 miles, your destination will be on your right.

The Bloedel Reserve (nature)
7571 NE Dolphin Drive, Bainbridge Island, Washington 98110

(206)842-7631

Tuesday–Sunday 10:00 a.m.–4:00 p.m.

$17

From Tacoma, head south on I-5 toward Portland. In 1.2 miles, take exit 132B to merge onto SR-16 West. In 0.5 miles, keep left to merge onto SR-16 West. In 26.0 miles, continue onto West SH-16. In 0.9 miles, merge onto SR-3 North. In 1.9 miles, keep left on SR-3 North toward Silverdale. In 16.0 miles, take exit onto SH-305 NE toward Kingston. In 0.4 miles, turn right onto SH-305 NE toward Kingston. In 7.2 miles, turn left onto Agatewood Road NE. In 0.3 miles, turn right onto NE Dolphin Drive. In 0.8 miles, your destination will be on your right.

Mount Rainier National Park (nature)
39000 SR-706 E, Ashford, Washington 98304

(360)569-2211

24-7

$30

From Seattle, head south on I-5. In 1.0 mile, take exit 154A to merge onto I-405 North toward Renton. In 2.0 miles, take exit 2 to merge onto SR-167 South toward Auburn. In 0.3 miles, keep right to merge onto SR-167 South toward Kent. In 20.0 miles, take a slight right turn to merge onto SR-161 South toward Puyallup. In 3.4 miles, take exit onto SR-161 South toward Eatonville. In 0.4 miles, turn left onto 31st Avenue SW toward Mt. Rainier. In 15.0 miles, keep left onto Meridian Avenue East. In 8.3 miles, turn left onto Center Street East. In 7.2 miles, turn left onto Mountain Highway East. In 4.9 miles, continue onto SR-706 East. In 14.0 miles, your destination will be on your left.

Golden Gardens Park (nature)
8498 Seaview Place NW, Seattle, Washington 98117

(206)684-4075

4:00 a.m.–11:30 p.m.

Free

From Tacoma, head north on I-5 toward Seattle. In 37.0 miles, take exit 172 onto North 85th Street toward Aurora Avenue North. In 3.6 miles, turn right onto 32nd Avenue NW. In 0.2 miles, keep left onto Golden Gardens Drive NW. In 0.6 miles, take a sharp left turn onto Seaview Place NW. In 0.2 miles, your destination will be on your right.

Kalaloch Tree of Life (nature)
101 Old State Road Highway, Forks, Washington 98331
24-7
Free
From Tacoma, head south on I-5. In 29.0 miles, take exit 104 to merge onto US-101 North toward Aberdeen. In 5.9 miles, continue onto SR-8 West toward Montesano. In 20.0 miles, merge onto SR-8 West. In 1.1 miles, continue onto US-12 West. In 11.0 miles, take exit toward Devonshire Road. In 900 feet, continue onto Wynoochee Valley Road. In 8.8 miles, turn left onto Wynoochee-Wishkah Road. In 4.6 miles, turn right onto Wishkah Road. In 2.1 miles, turn left onto Hoquiam Wishkah Road. In 1.7 miles, turn right onto East Hoquiam Road. In 5.2 miles, turn right onto US-101. In 56.0 miles, turn left onto Kalaloch Campground Road F. Prepare to park your vehicle. Once you make it to the beach from the trail, head right for your destination.

Manito Park (nature)
1702 S Grand Blvd, Spokane, Washington 99203
(509)625-6200
5:00 a.m.–11:00 p.m.
Free
From Kennewick, head north on US-395 toward Pasco. In 2.2 miles, keep right on I-182 toward Spokane. In 0.4 miles, keep left to merge onto I-182 East. In 1.4 miles, take exit 14 onto US-395 North toward Spokane. In 900 feet, keep left onto US-395 North. In 0.3 miles, keep right onto US-395 North. In 74.0 miles, continue onto I-90 East. In 60.0 miles, take exit 281 onto Division

Street. In 0.2 miles, turn right onto South Division Street. In 0.2 miles, turn right onto West Seventh Avenue. In 800 feet, turn left onto South McClellan Street. In 800 feet, turn left onto West Ninth Avenue. In 0.7 miles, turn right onto East 18th Avenue. In 800 feet, you will arrive at your destination.

Cape Disappointment State Park (nature)

244 Robert Gray Drive SW, Ilwaco, Washington 98624

(360)642-3078

10:00 a.m.–5:00 p.m.

$2.50

From Tacoma, head South on I-5 toward Portland. In 29.0 miles, take exit 104 to merge onto US-101 North toward Aberdeen. In 5.9 miles, continue onto SR-8 West. In 20.0 miles, merge onto SR-8 West. In 1.1 miles, continue onto US-12 West. In 10.0 miles, take exit toward Raymond. In 0.2 miles, turn left onto Main Street South. In 8.0 miles, turn left onto US-101. In 18.0 miles, at the roundabout, take the first exit onto US-101. In 30.0 miles, turn right onto US-101. In 13.0 miles, turn left onto Alt US-101. In 0.6 miles, turn right onto US-101. In 2.2 miles, turn left on Second Avenue SW. In 1.7 miles, take a slight left turn onto Coast Guard Road. In 0.5 miles, turn right onto Fort Canby Park Road. In 700 feet, turn left onto Fort Canby Park Road. In 400 feet, turn right onto Fort Canby Park Road. In 0.8 miles, turn right onto Fort Canby Park Road. In 0.3 miles, your destination will be on your left.

Gas Works Park (nature)

2101 N Northlake Way, Seattle, Washington 98130

(206)684-4075

6:00 a.m.–10:00 p.m.

Free

From Tacoma, head north on I-5 toward Seattle. In 32.0 miles, keep left on I-5 North. In 3.7 miles, take exit onto NE 42nd Street. In 800 feet, turn right onto 7th Avenue NE. In 0.2 miles, turn left onto 6th Avenue NE. In 450 feet, take a slight right turn onto NE Northlake Way. In 0.8 miles, turn left into the parking lot. You have arrived at your destination.

Washington Park Arboretum Botanical Gardens (nature)

2300 Arboretum Drive E, Seattle, Washington 98112

(206)543-8800

9:00 a.m.–5:00 p.m.

Free

From Tacoma, head north on I-5 toward Seattle. In 34.0 miles, take exit 168B to merge onto SR-520 East toward Kirkland. In 0.8 miles, take exit onto Montlake Boulevard. In 0.2 miles, continue onto East Lake Washington Boulevard. In 0.5 miles, turn left onto East Foster Lake Road. In 800 feet, turn right onto Arboretum Drive East. In 400 feet, you will arrive at your destination.

The Whale Museum (nature, ferry required)
62 First Street N, Friday Harbor, Washington 98250
(360)378-4710
10:00 a.m.–4:00 p.m.
$10
From Seattle, head north on I-5 toward Vancouver, B.C. In 64.0 miles, take exit 230 onto SR-20 toward Burlington. In 0.4 miles, turn left onto SR-20 toward San Juan. In 12.0 miles, keep right onto SR-20 Spur. In 2.8 miles, at the roundabout, take the first exit onto Commercial Avenue. In 1.3 miles, turn left onto 12th Street. In 2.7 miles, at the roundabout, take the second exit onto Oakes Avenue. In 0.4 miles, keep right onto Ferry Terminal Road. In 0.7 miles, take the Washington State ferry. In 19.0 miles, continue ahead. In 300 feet, turn right onto Front Street South. In 300 feet, take a sharp left turn onto Spring Street. In 40 feet, turn right onto Spring Street. In 250 feet, turn right onto First Street South. In 450 feet, your destination will be on your right.

Bellevue Botanical Gardens (nature)
12001 Main Street, Bellevue, Washington 98005
(425)452-2750
9:00 a.m.–5:00 p.m.
Free
From Tacoma, head north on I-5 toward Seattle. In 20.0 miles, take exit 154A to merge onto I-405 North toward Bellevue. In 600 feet, keep right to merge onto I-405 North. In 13.0 miles, take exit 12 onto 116th Avenue SE. In 800 feet, keep left onto 116th Avenue SE. In 0.2 miles, turn left onto 116th Avenue SE. In 0.2 miles, take a slight right turn onto SE first Street. In 900 feet, turn right onto Main Street. In 0.2 miles, turn right. In 100 feet, your destination will be on your right.

Volunteer Park (nature)
1247 15th Avenue E, Seattle, Washington 98112
(206)684-4075
6:00 a.m.–8:00 p.m.
Free

From Tacoma, head north on I-5 toward Seattle. In 34.0 miles, take exit 168A onto Lakeview Boulevard. In 700 feet, turn left onto Lakeview Boulevard East. In 500 feet, keep right onto Harvard Avenue East. In 900 feet, turn right onto East Boston Street. In 600 feet, turn right onto 10th Avenue East. In 0.7 miles, turn left onto East Prospect Street. In 0.2 miles, your destination will be on your left.

Rialto Beach (nature)
Mora Road, Forks, Washington 98331
(360)565-3100
24-7
Free
From Port Angeles, head west on US-101. In 55.0 miles, turn right onto La Push Road. In 3.1 miles, turn right onto Quillayute Road. In 5.9 miles, keep left onto Quillayute Road. In 0.9 miles, turn right onto Mora Road. In 2.8 miles, turn left. In 400 feet, prepare to park your vehicle. Your destination will be on your left.

Rhododendron Species Botanical Garden (nature)
2525 S 336th Street, Federal Way, Washington 98003
(253)838-4646
Tuesday–Sunday 10:00 a.m.–4:00 p.m.
$5
From Tacoma, head north on I-5 toward Settle. In 8.0 miles, take exit 142A to merge onto SR-18 East toward Auburn. In 0.6 miles, take the exit onto Weyerhaeuser Way South. In 0.3 miles, turn left onto Weyerhaeuser Way South. In 0.4 miles, at the roundabout, take the second exit onto Weyerhaeuser Way South. In 700 feet, turn left onto Weyerhaeuser Road. In 0.8 miles, turn left. In 0.3 miles, your destination will be on your left.

Beacon Rock State Park (nature)
34841 WA-14, Stevenson, Washington 98648
(509)427-8265
8:00 a.m.–10:00 p.m.
$5
From Tacoma, head south on I-5 toward Portland. In 126.0 miles, take exit 7 to merge onto I-205 South toward Salem. In 10.0 miles, take exit 27 to merge onto SR-14 East toward Camas. In 700 feet, keep left to merge onto SR-14 East. In 11.0 miles, at the roundabout, take the second exit onto SR-14. In 17.0 miles, take a slight left turn onto Kueffler Road. In 250 feet, you will arrive at your destination.

Wallace Falls State Park (nature)
14503 Wallace Lake Road, Gold Bar, Washington 98251
(360)793-0420
24-7
$10
From Seattle, head east on I-90 toward Spokane. In 6.9 miles, take exit 10A to merge onto I-405 North toward Everett. In 0.5 miles, keep left to merge onto I-405 North toward Spokane. In 12.0 miles, take exit 23 to merge onto SR-522 toward Woodinville. In 0.9 miles, keep right to merge onto SR-522 East. In 13.0 miles, keep right onto US-2 East toward Wenatchee. In 10.0 miles, at the roundabout, take the second exit onto US-2 East. In 3.7 miles, turn left onto First Street West. In 0.4 miles, turn right onto May Creek Road. In 1.1 miles, turn left onto Wallace Lake Road. Your destination will be on your right.

Kubota Garden (nature)
9817 55th Avenue S, Seattle, Washington 98118
(206)725-5060
6:00 a.m.–10:00 p.m.
Free
From Tacoma, head north on I-5 toward Seattle. In 24.0 miles, take exit 157 onto ML King Way. In 0.3 miles, keep right onto ML King Way. In 0.4 miles, turn right onto South Ryan Way. In 0.5 miles, turn left onto 51st Avenue South. In 0.5 miles, turn right onto South Roxbury Street. In 90 feet, take a slight right turn onto Renton Avenue South. In 0.3 miles, turn right onto 55th Avenue South. In 300 feet, your destination will be on your right.

Snoqualmie Falls
6501 Railroad Avenue SE, Fall City, Washington 98065
(360)421-5849
10:00 a.m.–7:00 p.m.
$5 parking fee
From Seattle, take I-90 east toward Spokane. In 23.0 miles, take exit 25 onto SR-18 West toward Snoqualmie Parkway. In 0.3 miles, turn left onto SR-18 toward Snoqualmie Parkway. In 800 feet, continue onto Echo Glen Road. In 3.6 miles, turn left onto Railroad Avenue SE. In 0.3 miles, at the roundabout, take the third exit onto Railroad Avenue SE. In 0.2 miles, turn left. In 50 feet, turn left. In 200 feet, your destination will be on your right.

Elandan Gardens/Thousand-year-old bonsai tree (nature)
3050 W SH-16 E, Bremerton, Washington 98312
(360)373-8260
Tuesday–Sunday 10:00 a.m.–5:00 p.m.
$8
From Tacoma, head south on I-5 toward Portland. In 1.2 miles, take exit 132B to merge onto SR-16. In 0.5 miles, keep left onto SR-16 West. In 26.0 miles, continue onto Werst SH-16. In 700 feet, your destination will be on your right.

Ginkgo Petrified Forest/Wanapum Recreation Area (nature)

4511 Huntzinger Road, Vantage, Washington 98950

(509)856-2700

10:00 a.m.–5:00 p.m.

$10

From Seattle, head east on I-90 toward Spokane. In 108.0 miles, keep left on I-90 East. In 26.0 miles, take exit 136 toward Vantage. In 0.2 miles, turn left onto Wanapum Road. In 0.4 miles, your destination will be on your left.

Mima Mounds Natural Area Preserve (nature)

12315 Waddell Creek Road, SW, Olympia, WA 98512

(360)902-1434

8:30 a.m.–5:30 p.m.

$10

From Tacoma, head south on I-5 toward Portland. In 39.0 miles, take exit 95 onto SR-121 North toward Littlerock. In 3.8 miles, turn right onto Waddell Creek Road SW. In 0.8 miles, turn left. In 0.3 miles, turn right. In 100 feet, your destination will be on your right.

Overgrown Ship Hulk (nature)

3011 Oakes Avenue, Anacortes, Washington 98221

Sunrise to sunset

Free

From Seattle, head north on I-5 toward Vancouver, B.C. In 64.0 miles, take exit 230 onto SR-20 toward Vancouver, B.C. In 0.4 miles, turn left onto SR-20 toward San Juan. In 12.0 miles, keep right onto SR-20 Spur. In 2.8 miles, at the roundabout, take the first exit onto Commercial Avenue. In 1.3 miles, turn left onto 12th Street. In 1.5 miles, take a take right into the parking lot, head down to the beach. Your destination will be on your right.

The Arctic Club of Seattle (historical)

700 3rd Avenue, Seattle, WA 98104

(206)340-0340

24-7

Free to look

From Tacoma, head north on I-5 toward Seattle. In 30.0 miles, take exit 164 toward Madison Street. In 800 feet, keep left onto Dearborn Street. In 0.3 miles, keep left onto 7th Avenue. In 0.7 miles, keep right toward Madison Street. In 0.3 miles, turn left onto Madison Street. In 0.3 miles, turn left onto 2nd Avenue. In 900 feet, turn left onto Cherry Street. In 450 feet, your destination will be on your left.

Okanogan Ghost Town/Molson Historical Society (historical; winter months, four-wheel drive required)
5309 Molson Road, Oroville, Washington 98844
(509)485-3266
Tuesday–Sunday 10:00 a.m.–5:00 p.m.
$14
From Spokane, head west on I-90. In 2.3 miles, take exit 277 onto US-2 West toward Davenport. In 600 feet, keep left onto US-2 West. In 3.8 miles, at the roundabout, take the second exit onto West Sunset Highway. In 2.8 miles, at the roundabout, take the first exit onto West Sunset Highway. In 56.0 miles, turn right onto SR-21. In 0.5 miles, continue onto SR-174. In 19.0 miles, take a slight right turn onto Spokane Way. In 0.3 miles, take a slight right turn onto Federal Avenue. In 0.3 miles, turn right onto SR-155. In 2.0 miles, turn right onto SR-155. In 0.2 miles, turn left onto River Drive. In 51.0 miles, turn left onto South Dayton Street. In 0.3 miles, turn left onto US-97. In 24.0 miles, keep left onto South Whitcomb Avenue. In 15.0 miles, take a slight right turn onto Eastside Oroville Road. In 2.0 miles, turn right onto Chesaw Road. In 8.2 miles, turn left onto Molson Road. In 5.2 miles, your destination will be on your left.

Fort Worden Historical Park (historical) (ferry required)
200 Battery Way, Port Townsend, Washington 98368
(360)344-4400
7:00 a.m.–8:00 p.m.
$30
From Seattle, head north on I-5 toward Vancouver, B.C. In 12.0 miles, take exit 177 onto SR-104 West toward Edmonds. In 700 feet, keep left onto SR-104 West toward Kingston Ferry. In 0.3 miles, keep right onto SR-104 West toward Edmonds. In 0.2 miles, turn right onto Lake Ballinger Way. In 1.0 mile, keep right onto Edmonds Way. In 2.4 miles, take a slight right turn onto Edmonds Way. In 1.3 miles, turn left onto Main Street. In 0.2 miles, take the Washington State ferry. In 5.6 miles, continue ahead. In 400 feet, take a slight right turn onto NE SH-104. In 4.0 miles, turn right onto SH-104 NE. In 5.0 miles, turn right onto Hood Canal Floating Bridge. In 1.7 miles, turn right onto Paradise Bay Road. In 6.0 miles, turn right onto Oak Bay Road. In 6.9 miles, keep left onto Oak Bay Road. In 3.7 miles, turn right onto Rhody Drive. In 3.4 miles, continue onto SR-20. In 2.5 miles, at the roundabout, take the third exit onto Rainier Street. In 0.4 miles, at the roundabout, take the first exit onto Discovery Road. In 0.9 miles, take a slight left turn onto Discovery Road. In 1.0 mile, turn left onto Cherry Street. In 0.4 miles, take a slight right turn onto Cherry Street. In 0.4 miles, you will arrive at your destination.

Northern State Recreation Area/Hospital Ruins (historical)

Helmick Road, Sedro Woolley, Washington 98284

(360)416-1350

24-7

Free

From Seattle, head north on I-5. In 67.0 miles, take exit 232 onto Cook Road toward Sedro-Woolley. In 0.2 miles, turn right onto Cook Road. In 4.2 miles, at the roundabout, take the second exit onto Cook Road. In 700 feet, take the roundabout. Take the third exit onto SR-9 North. In 0.3 miles, at the roundabout, take the second exit onto West Moore Street. In 2.5 miles, turn left onto Helmick Road. In 0.5 miles, your destination will be on your left.

Jimi Hendrix Memorial (historical)

350 Monroe Avenue NE, Renton, Washington 98056

(425)255-1511

4:00 a.m.–11:30 p.m.

Free

From Tacoma, head north on I-5 toward Seattle. In 20.0 miles, take exit 154A to merge onto I-405 North toward Bellevue. In 600 feet, keep right to merge onto I-405 North toward Renton. In 3.7 miles, take exit 4 onto SR-169 South toward SR-900 West. In 0.2 miles, keep left toward Bronson Way. In 0.4 miles, turn right onto Sunset Boulevard North. In 0.2 miles, turn right onto NE Third Street. In 1.0 mile, turn right onto Monroe Avenue NE. In 700 feet, your destination will be on your left.

Merchants Café and Saloon (historical)
109 Yesler Way, Seattle, WA 98104
(206)467-5070
Friday–Saturday 11:00 a.m.–2:00 a.m.; Sunday–Thursday 11:00 a.m.–12:00 a.m.
Free to look
From Tacoma, head north on I-5 toward Seattle. In 30.0 miles, take exit 164A onto James Street. In 800 feet, keep left onto Dearborn Street toward James Street. In 0.3 miles, keep left onto James Street. In 0.6 miles, take a slight right turn onto James Street. In 0.2 miles, turn left onto Yesler Way. In 100 feet, your destination will be on your right.

Oregon

Goonies Jail/Oregon Film Museum (obscure)
732 Duane Street, Astoria Oregon 97013
(503)325-2203
10:00 a.m.–4:00 p.m.
$5
From Portland, head west on US-26 toward Beaverton. In 73.0 miles, take a slight right turn onto US-101 North toward Astoria. In 19.0 miles, at the roundabout, take the second exit onto West Marine Drive. In 0.5 miles, continue onto West Marine Drive. In 1.0 mile, turn right onto Duane Street. In 200 feet, your destination will be on your right.

Local Shoe Tree (obscure)
199 US-26, Mitchell, Oregon 97750
24-7
Free (pair of shoes as offering)
From Bend, head north on US-97 toward Redmond. In 16.0 miles, turn right onto SE Evergreen Avenue. In 15.0 miles, keep left onto OR-126. In 0.3 miles, at the roundabout, take the second exit onto OR-126. In 2.3 miles, continue onto NW 3rd Street. In 48.0 miles, your destination will be on your left.

Shallon Whey Winery (obscure)
1598 Duane Streeet, Astoria, Oregon 97103
(503)325-5978
1:00 p.m.–6:00 p.m.
$23+ (wine tasting)
From Portland, head west on US-26 toward Beaverton. In 73.0 miles, take a slight right turn onto US-101 North toward Astoria. In 19.0 miles, at the roundabout, take the second exit onto West Marine Drive. In 0.5 miles, continue onto West Marine Drive. In 1.0 mile, turn left onto Commercial Street. In 0.4 miles, turn right onto 16th Street. In 100 feet, your destination will be on your right.

Wax Works Museum (obscure)
250 SW Bay Boulevard, Newport, Oregon 97365
(541)265-2206
10:00 a.m.–5:00 p.m.
$15
From Portland, head south on I-5 toward Salem. In 72.0 miles, take exit 228 onto OR-34 toward Corvallis. In 0.3 miles, turn right onto Highway 34 SE. In 9.6 miles, turn left onto OR-34. In 1.0 mile, continue onto Corvallis-Newport Highway. In 30.0 miles, continue straight. In 4.5 miles, continue onto US-20. In 14.0 miles, turn left onto SE Benton Street. In 0.2 miles, turn left onto SW Hatfield Drive. In 0.2 miles, turn right onto SW Bay Boulevard. Your destination will be on your right.

The Grotto Shrine (obscure)
8840 NE Skidmore Street, Portland, Oregon 97220
(503)254-7371
9:00 a.m.–6:30 p.m.
$6

From Salem, head north on I-5 toward Portland. In 35.0 miles, take exit 288 to merge onto I-205 North toward Oregon City. In 23.0 miles, take exit 23A onto Sandy Boulevard. In 0.4 miles, turn right onto NE 97th Avenue. In 0.2 miles, turn right onto NE Prescott Street. In 0.3 miles turn left onto NE 92nd Avenue. In 700 feet, turn right onto NE Skidmore Street. In 800 feet, your destination will be on your left.

The Hat Museum (obscure)

1928 SE Ladd Avenue, Portland, Oregon 97214
(503)232-0433
Friday–Saturday 10:00 a.m.–2:30 p.m.
$35
From Salem, head north on I-5 toward Portland. In 40.0 miles, take exit 299B to merge onto I-405 North toward City Center. In 0.3 miles, take exit 1A to merge onto South Harbor Drive. In 0.7 miles, turn right onto SW Naito Parkway. In 500 feet, take a slight right turn toward Hawthorne Bridge. In 350 feet, take a slight right turn onto SE Hawthorne Boulevard. In 1.0 mile, turn right onto SE Ladd Avenue. In 0.3 miles, your destination will be on your left.

Kam Wah Chung & Company Museum (obscure)

125 W Canton Street, John Day, Oregon 97845
(541) 575-2800
9:00 a.m.–5:00 p.m.
Donation
From Bend, head north on US-97 toward Redmond. In 15.0 miles, turn right onto SE Evergreen Avenue. In 15.0 miles, keep left onto OR-126. In 0.3 miles, at the roundabout, take the second exit onto OR-126. In 2.3 miles, continue onto NW Third Street. In 117.0 miles, turn left onto NW Canton Street. In 250 feet, your destination will be on your right.

The Last Blockbuster Store (obscure)

211 NE Revere Avenue, Bend, Oregon 97701
(541)385-9111
Sunday–Thursday 10:30 a.m.–8:00 p.m.; Friday–Saturday 10:30 a.m.–9:00 p.m.
Free
From Redmond, head south on US-97. In 1.4 miles, continue onto The Dalles-California Highway. In 12.0 miles, keep left onto North Highway 97. In 2.1 miles, take exit 137 onto Revere Avenue. In 0.2 miles, turn left onto NW Revere Avenue. In 0.3 miles, turn right. Your destination will be on your right.

Rimsky-Korsakoffee House (coffee; obscure)
707 SE 12th Avenue, Portland, Oregon 97214
(503)232-2640
Free to look
From Eugene, head north on I-5 toward Portland. In 106.0 miles, keep right onto I-5. In 1.1 miles, take exit 300 to merge onto I-84 East. In 0.2 miles, take exit toward OMSI. In 600 feet, turn right onto SE Water Avenue. In 250 feet, turn left onto SE Taylor Street. In 0.2 miles, turn left onto Grand Avenue. In 500 feet, turn right onto SE Belmont Street. In 0.3 miles, turn left onto SE 12th Avenue. In 450 feet, your destination will be on your left.

Treehouse Ziplines and Treesort (obscure)
300 Page Creek Road, Cave Junction, Oregon 97523
(541)592-2208
9:00 a.m.–5:00 p.m.
$65+ (zipline) $15 (horse ride) $150+ (treehouse rental)
From Eugene, head south on I-5. In 136.0 miles, take exit 55 onto US-199 toward Crescent City. In 0.5 miles, turn right onto Grants Pass Parkway. In 31.0 miles, turn left onto Rockydale Road. In 6.6 miles, turn left onto Waldo Road. In 0.8 miles, turn right onto Takilma Road. In 2.4 miles, turn left onto Page Creek Road. In 0.2 miles, your destination will be on your left.

The Oregon Vortex Mystery House (obscure)
4303 Left Fork Sardine Creek Road, Goldhill, Oregon 97525
(541)855-1543
9:00 a.m.–5:00 p.m.
$13.75
From Eugene, head south on I-5. In 149.0 miles, take exit 43 onto OR-234 toward Goldhill. In 0.2 miles, turn left onto Main Street. In 0.2 miles, turn right onto Rouge River Highway. In 1.0 mile, turn left onto Sardine Creek Road. In 4.3 miles, your destination will be on your left.

Enchanted Forest Amusement Park (obscure)
8462 Enchanted Way SE, Turner, Oregon 97392
(503)363-3060
Sunday–Monday, Thursday–Saturday 10:30 a.m.–6:00 p.m.
$12
From Eugene, head north on I-5 toward Portland. In 51.0 miles, take exit 244 toward North Jefferson. In 0.2 miles, turn right onto Jefferson Highway. In 250 feet, turn left onto Enchanted Way SE. In 3.0 miles, turn right into the parking lot. In 200 feet, you will arrive at your destination.

Multnomah Falls (nature)
Corbett, Oregon 97019
(503)695-2376
8:00 a.m.–9:00 p.m.
Free
From Portland, head east on I-84 toward The Dalles. In 29.0 miles, take exit 31 toward Multnomah Falls. In 0.2 miles, prepare to park your vehicle. Head right. In 90 feet, walk through the tunnel on the right. In 300 feet, your destination will be on your left.

Petersen Rock Garden & Museum (nature)
7930 SW 77th Street, Redmond, Oregon 97756
(541)382-5574
9:00 a.m.–5:00 p.m.
$4.50

From Bend, take US-97 north toward Redmond. In 8.0 miles, turn left onto 61st Street. In 1.1 miles, turn left onto SW Young Avenue. In 1.0 mile, turn right onto SW 77th Street. In 0.5 miles, turn right. Your destination will be on your left.

Thor's Well (nature; hiking required)
Highway 101 Cape Perpetua Area, Yachts, Oregon 97498
24-7
Free
From Eugene, head north on I-5 toward Portland. In 34.0 miles, take exit 228 onto OR-34 toward Corvallis. In 0.3 miles, turn left onto Highway 34 SE toward Linn. In 9.8 miles, turn left onto OR-34. In 1.0 mile, continue onto Corvallis-Newport Highway. In 30.0 miles, continue ahead. In 4.5 miles, continue onto US-20. In 14.0 miles, turn left onto SW Coast Highway. In 27.0 miles, prepare to park your vehicle near Captain Cook. Take a right onto Captain Cook. In 180 feet, take a slight left turn onto Captain Cook. In 0.2 miles, your destination will be on your left.

Hug Point State Recreation Site (nature; be careful of tide)
Beach Access Road, Arch Cape, Oregon 97102
(800)551-6949
Monday–Friday 8:00 a.m.–5:00 p.m.
Free
From Portland, head west on US-26 toward Beaverton. In 74.0 miles, continue onto US-101. In 8.6 miles, turn right onto Hug Point. In 400 feet, your destination will be on your right.

Clear Lake (nature)
McKenzie Highway, Foster, Oregon 97759
Daily
Free
From Portland, head south on I-5 toward Salem. In 46.0 miles, take exit 253 to merge onto OR-22 toward Bend. In 0.3 miles, turn left to merge onto OR-22. In 13.0 miles, continue onto North Santiam Highway SE. In 67.0 miles, turn right onto OR-22. In 400 feet, continue onto Santiam Highway. In 3.1 miles, turn left. In 3.7 miles, turn left onto Forest Service Road 775. In 0.4 miles, keep right. In 300 feet, prepare to park your vehicle. Head left onto Clear Lake. In 200 feet, you will arrive at your destination.

Oregon Caves National Monument and Preserve (nature)
19000 Caves Highway, Cave Junction, Oregon 97523
(541) 592-2100
9:30 a.m.–4:00 p.m. (closed during the winter)
Free
From Eugene, head south on I-5. In 136.0 miles, take exit 55 onto US-199 toward Crescent City. In 0.5 miles, turn right onto Grants Pass. In 29.0 miles, turn left onto Laurel Road. In 2.2 miles, turn left onto OR-46. In 12.0 miles, turn left onto OR-46. In 6.0 miles, take a slight left turn. You have arrived at your destination.

Prehistoric Gardens Dinosaur Park (nature)
36848 US Highway 101, Port Orford, OR 97465
(541)332-4463
10:00 a.m.–6:00 p.m.
$12
From Eugene, head south on I-5. In 30.0 miles, take exit 162 onto OR-38. In 6.6 miles, turn right onto West B Avenue. In 34.0 miles, keep left onto OR-38. In 16.0 miles, continue onto Umpqua Avenue. In 0.3 miles, turn left onto US-101. In 24.0 miles, continue onto Tremont Avenue. In 24.0 miles, continue onto Tremont Avenue. In 3.4 miles, continue onto Evans Boulevard. In 0.5 miles, keep right onto US-101 South. In 4.8 miles, keep right onto US-101 South. In 18.0 miles, continue onto US-101. In 27.0 miles, continue onto US-101. In 12.0 miles, your destination will be on your right.

Newberry National Volcanic Monument (nature; hiking required)
La Pine, Oregon 97739
(541) 593-2421
Daily
$5
From Bend, head south on US-97. In 17.0 miles, turn left onto Paulina-East Lake Road. In 9.5 miles, turn left. In 800 feet, turn right. In 15 feet, prepare to park your vehicle near Newberry 11.

Proxy Falls (nature; hiking required)
OR-242, McKenzie Bridge, Oregon 97413
Daily (closed during the winter)
Free
From Bend, head north on US-97 toward Redmond. In 2.3 miles, take a slight right turn onto US-20 West toward Sisters. In 20.0 miles, turn left onto McKenzie Highway. In 28.0 miles, prepare to park your vehicle. Head left onto Proxy Falls. In 0.55 miles, you will arrive at your destination.

Painted Hills (nature; hiking required)
32651 Highway 19, Kimberley, Oregon 97848
(541)987-2333
Daily
Free
From Bend, head north on US-97 toward Redmond. In 15.0 miles, turn right onto SE Evergreen Avenue. In 15.0 miles, keep left onto OR-126. In 0.3 miles, at the roundabout, take the second exit onto OR-126. In 2.3 miles, continue onto NW Third Street. In 44.0 miles, turn left onto Burnt Ranch Road. In 5.6 miles, turn left onto Bear Creek Road. In 0.4 miles, turn right onto Bear Creek Road. In 1.2 miles, prepare to park your vehicle near Bear Creek Road. You have arrived at your destination.

Crater Lake (nature; hiking required)
Lighting Spring Trail, Chiloquin, Oregon 97624
(541)594-3000
Open May–September 9:30 a.m.–5:00 p.m. (closed during winter); June/September 9:30 a.m.–5:00 p.m.; October 10:00 a.m.–4:00 p.m.
$30
From Bend, head south on US-97. In 53.0 miles, take a slight right turn. In 450 feet, keep right. In 3.0 miles, turn right onto OR-62. In 8.5 miles, keep right onto OR-62. In 16.0 miles, turn right. In 6.8 miles, turn right. In 200 feet, your destination will be on your left.

Octopus Tree (nature)
Cape Meares Lighthouse Drive, Tillamook, Oregon 97141
(800)551-6949
7:00 a.m.–8:00 p.m.
From Portland, head west on US-26 toward Beaverton. In 21.0 miles, stay left onto NW Wilson River Highway. In 51.0 miles, turn left onto Main Avenue. In 500 feet, turn right onto Third Street. In 8.3 miles, turn right onto Netarts Highway West. In 0.6 miles, turn right onto Cape Meares Loop. In 2.5 miles, turn left onto Lighthouse Road. In 0.4 miles, your destination will be on your left.

Salt Creek Falls (nature)
Blue River, Oregon 97413
Sunrise to sunset
Free
From Bend, take US-97 south. In 40.0 miles, turn right onto Crescent Cut-off Road. In 12.0 miles, turn right onto OR-58. In 16.0 miles, turn left onto Forest Service Road 5893. In 70 feet, the destination is on your right.

Neskowin Ghost Forest/Proposal Rock (nature)
49110 Proposal Rock Loop, Neskowin, Oregon 97149
(800)551-6949
Daily
Free
From Salem, head west on OR-22. In 26.0 miles, continue onto Salmon River Highway. In 26.0 miles, take a slight right turn onto US-101 North toward Astoria. In 0.2 miles, turn right onto

Oregon Coast Highway. In 6.7 miles, turn left onto South Beach Road. In 800 feet, turn right onto Proposal Rock Loop. In 150 feet, keep left onto Proposal Rock Loop. In 0.2 miles, turn right onto Proposal Rock Loop. In 150 feet, your destination will be on your left.

Crack in the Ground (nature; hiking required; four-wheel drive recommended)
Christmas Valley, Oregon 97641
Daily
Free
From Bend Parkway in Bend, take US-97 south. In 25.0 miles, turn left onto Fremont Highway. In 29.0 miles, turn left onto CR-5-10. In 22.0 miles, turn left onto Christmas Valley Highway. In 12.0 miles, turn left onto Crack in the Ground Road. In 6.3 miles, prepare to park your vehicle. Your destination will be on your right.

Darlingtonia State Natural Site (nature)
5400 Mercer Lake Road, Florence, Oregon 97439
(800)551-6949
24-7
Free
From Eugene, head west on 11th Avenue. In 45.0 miles, turn left onto OR-126. In 14.0 miles, take a slight right turn. In 300 feet, take a slight right turn onto US-101. In 5.0 miles, turn right onto Mercer Lake Road. In 500 feet, your destination will be on your right.

Devils Punchbowl State Park (nature)

Otter Rock, Oregon 97369
(800)551-6949
9:00 a.m.–6:00 p.m.
Free

From Eugene, head north on I-5 toward Portland. In 60.0 miles, take exit 299 onto Macadam Avenue toward Detroit. In 0.2 miles, turn left onto OR-22. In 0.6 miles, continue onto Mission Street SE. In 1.7 miles, take a slight right turn onto OR-22 West. In 0.3 miles, take a slight left turn onto Bellevue Street SE. In 1.2 miles, take a slight right turn onto OR-22 west. In 0.4 miles, keep left onto OR-22 West. In 26.0 miles, continue onto Salmon River Highway. In 27.0 miles, continue onto North Highway 101. In 22.0 miles, turn right onto Otter Crest Loop. In 400 feet, turn left onto Otter Crest Loop. In 100 feet, turn left onto Otter Crest Loop. In 0.2 miles, turn right onto First Street. In 0.4 miles, you will arrive at your destination.

Toketee Falls (nature)

1121 Houser Court, Idleyld Park, Oregon 97447
(541)957-3200
Sunrise to sunset
Free

From Bend, head south on US-97. In 50.0 miles, keep left onto Highway 97 North. In 18.0 miles, turn right onto East Diamond Lake Highway. In 44.0 miles, turn right onto Toketee School Road. In 0.2 miles, take a slight right turn onto Toketee School Road. In 250 feet, turn left onto Toketee Village Loop. In 200 feet, your destination will be on your left.

Fort Rock (nature)
77417 Cow Cave Road Lane, Fort Rock, Oregon 97735
(503)986-0707
Daily
Free
From Bend, take US-97 south. In 25.0 miles, turn left onto Fremont Highway. In 29.0 miles, turn left onto CR-5-10. In 6.4 miles, turn left onto CR-5-11. In 1.0 mile, turn left onto Cow Cave Lane. In 0.3 miles, you will arrive at your destination.

Metolius Balancing Rocks (nature; hiking required)
Cove Palisades State Park, Culver, Oregon 97734
Daily
Free
From Bend, head north on US-97 toward Redmond. In 32.0 miles, take a slight left turn onto SW Culver Highway. In 2.3 miles, turn left onto SW Iris Lane. In 1.0 mile, turn right onto SW Feather Drive. In 1.2 miles, turn left on SW Fisch Lane. In 0.5 miles, turn left onto SW Frazier Drive. In 0.5 miles, turn left onto SW Peck Road. In 9.4 miles, take a slight left turn onto SW Jordan Road. In 1.2 miles, turn right onto SW Jordan Road. In 1.0 mile, turn left onto SW Graham Road. In 7.8 miles, prepare to park your vehicle near Montgomery Road. Your destination will be to your right.

Haystack Rock (nature; hiking required)

Haystack Rock, Cannon Beach, Oregon 97110

(503)436-2623

Open 24 hours

Free

From Portland, head west on US-26 toward Beaverton. In 74.0 miles, continue onto US-101. In 4.4 miles, stay right onto Sunset Boulevard. In 0.2 miles, turn left onto South Hemlock Street. In 250 feet, stay right onto Forest Lawn Road. In 900 feet, prepare to park your vehicle near Forest Lawn Road.

Rice Northwest Museum of Rocks and Minerals (nature)

26385 NW Groveland Drive, Hillsboro, Oregon 97124

(503)647-2418

Wednesday–Friday 1:00 p.m.–5:00 p.m.; Saturday–Sunday 10:00 a.m.–5:00 p.m.

$10

From Portland, head west on US-26 toward Beaverton. In 13.0 miles, take exit 61B onto Helvetia Road. In 0.5 miles, turn left. In 0.4 miles, turn right onto NW Groveland Drive. In 1.1 miles, turn right. In 600 feet, turn right. In 500 feet, your destination will be on your right.

Crystal Springs Rhododendron Garden (nature)

5801 SE 28th Avenue, Portland, Oregon 97202

(503)267-7509

Tuesday, Thursday–Sunday 10:00 a.m.–4:00 p.m.; Wednesday 1:00 p.m.–4:00 p.m.

From Eugene, head north on I-5 toward Portland. In 105.0 miles, take exit 299 A oot Macadam Avenue. In 0.7 miles, take a slight left turn onto South Macadam Avenue. In 0.2 miles, take a slight right turn onto South Whitaker Street. In 300 feet, turn right onto South Kelly Avenue. In 700 feet, take a slight right turn onto SW Ross Island Bridge. In 0.6 miles, take a slight right turn onto OR-99 East South toward Milwaukie. In 2.3 miles, turn right onto SE 23rd Avenue. In 400 feet, turn right onto SE Bybee Road. In 0.7 miles, turn left onto SE 28th Avenue. In 600 feet, your destination will be on your left.

International Rose Test Garden (nature)

400 SW Kingston Avenue, Portland, Oregon 97205

(503)823-3636

7:30 a.m.–9:00 p.m.

Free

From Eugene, head north on I-5 toward Portland. In 98.0 miles, take exit 292A to merge onto OR-217 North toward Tigard. In 7.5 miles, take exit onto Barnes Road. In 700 feet, keep right onto Barnes Road East. In 3.6 miles, take a slight right turn. In 0.6 miles, turn left onto SW Rose Garden Way. In 150 feet, you will arrive at your destination.

Smith Rock State Park (nature)
9241 NE Crooked River Drive, Terrebonne, Oregon 97760
(541)548-7501
7:00 a.m.–7:00 p.m.
$5
From Bend, head north on US-97 toward Redmond. In 22.0 miles, turn right onto NW Smith Rock Way. In 0.6 miles, turn left on NE First Street. In 2.0 miles, turn left onto NE Crooked River Drive. In 1.1 miles, your destination will be on your right.

Hoyt Arboretum (nature)
4000 SW Fairview Boulevard, Portland, Oregon 97221
(503)865-8733
5:30 a.m.–9:00 p.m.
Free
From Eugene, head north on I-5. In 98.0 miles, take exit 292A to merge onto OR-217 North toward Tigard. In 7.2 miles, take exit to merge onto US-26 East toward Portland. In 900 feet, keep left to merge onto SW Sunset Highway. In 2.9 miles, take exit 72. In 700 feet, turn left onto SW Canyon Road. In 900 feet, keep left. In 800 feet, you will arrive at your destination.

John Day Fossil Beds National Monument (nature)
32651 OR-19, Kimberly, Oregon 97848
(541)987-2333
Sunrise to sunset
Free
From Bend, head north on US-97 toward Redmond. In 15.0 miles, turn right onto SE Evergreen Avenue. In 15.0 miles, keep left onto OR-126. In 0.3 miles, at the roundabout, take the second exit onto OR-126. In 2.3 miles, continue onto NW Third Street. In 44.0 miles, turn left onto Burnt Ranch Road. In 5.6 miles, turn left onto Bear Creek Road, your destination will be on your right.

Portland Japanese Garden (nature)
611 SW Kingston Avenue, Portland, Oregon 97205

(503)223-1321
Wednesday–Monday 10:00 a.m.–3:30 p.m.
$18.95
From Eugene, head north on I-5 toward Portland. In 98.0 miles, take exit 292A to merge onto OR-217 North toward Tigard. In 7.5 miles, keep right onto Barnes Road East. In 700 feet, keep right onto Barnes Road East. In 3.6 miles, take a slight right turn. In 0.5 miles, turn right into the parking lot. You have arrived at your destination.

Latourell Falls (nature)

42746 NE Latourell Road, Corbett, Oregon 97019
(800)452-5687
6:00 a.m.–10:00 p.m.
Free
From Portland, head east on I-84 toward The Dalles. In 26.0 miles, take exit 28 onto Historic Route 30 toward Bridal Veil. In 0.5 miles, turn right. In 150 feet, turn right onto East Historic Columbia River Highway. In 2.8 miles, take a sharp left turn. You have arrived at your destination.

Sea Lion Cave (nature)

91560 Highway 101, Florence, Oregon 97439

(541)547-3111

9:00 a.m.–5:00 p.m.

$14

From Eugene, head west on 11th Avenue. In 45.0 miles, turn left onto OR-126. In 14.0 miles, take a slight right turn. In 300 feet, take a slight right turn onto US-101. In 11.0 miles, your destination will be on your left.

The Oregon Botanical Garden (nature)

879 W Main Street, Silverton, Oregon 97381

(503)874-8100

Wednesday–Sunday 10:00 a.m.–3:00 p.m.

$8-$12

From Portland, head south on I-5 toward Salem. In 18.0 miles, take exit 282A onto OR-551 toward Canby. In 5.9 miles, continue onto OR-99E South. In 5.3 miles, turn left onto Young Street. In 6.8 miles, take a slight left turn onto Hillsboro Silverton Highway. In 4.1 miles, turn right onto East C Street. In 600 feet, continue onto West C Street. In 0.4 miles, continue onto Westfield Street. In 0.5 miles, turn right onto West Main Street. In 0.2 miles, turn left. In 0.3 miles, turn right. In 250 feet, you will arrive at your destination.

Bridal Veil Falls (nature)

46249 E Historic Columbia River Highway, Corbett, Oregon 97019

(503)695-2261

6:00 a.m.–10:00 p.m.

Free

From Portland, head east on I-84 toward The Dalles. In 26.0 miles, take exit 28 onto Historic Route 30 toward Bridal Veil. In 0.5 miles, take a sharp right turn. In 250 feet, turn right onto East Historic Columbia River Highway. In 0.8 miles, your destination will be on your right.

Oregon Dunes National Recreation Area (nature)

855 US-101, Reedsport, Oregon 97467

(541)271-6000

8:00 a.m.–6:30 p.m.

$5

From Eugene, head south on I-5. In 30.0 miles, take exit 162 onto OR-99 South toward Drain. In 6.6 miles, turn right onto West B Avenue. In 34.0 miles, stay left onto OR-38. In 16.0 miles, continue onto Umpqua Avenue. In 0.3 miles, turn left onto US-101. In 150 feet, your destination will be on your left.

Lan Su Chinese Garden (nature)

239 NW Everett Street, Portland, Oregon 97209

(503)228-8131

10:00 a.m.–4:00 p.m.

$12.95

From Eugene, head north on I-5 toward Portland. In 106.0 miles, take exit 299B to merge onto I-405 North toward City Center. In 0.3 miles, keep right on I-405 North. In 1.9 miles, take exit 2B toward Everett Street. In 900 feet, turn right onto NW Everett Street. In 0.6 miles, your destination will be on your left.

Lava River Cave State Park (nature)

US Highway 97, Bend, Oregon 97702

(541)593-2421

9:00 a.m.–4:00 p.m.

$5

From Bend, head South on US-97. In 4.4 miles, take exit toward Lava Lands Visitor Center. In 700 feet, turn left. In 1.2 miles, turn right. In 300 feet, your destination will be on your left.

Wooden Shoe Tulip Farm (nature)
33814 South Meridian Road, Woodburn, Oregon 97071
(503)634-2243
10:00 a.m.–4:00 p.m.
Free to look
From Portland, take I-5 south toward Salem. In 18.0 miles, take exit 282A onto OR-551 toward Canby. In 5.9 miles, continue onto OR-99E South. In 1.9 miles, turn left onto G Street. In 800 feet, stay left onto J Street. In 2.9 miles, turn right onto South Meridian Road. In 3.4 miles, turn left onto South Meridian Road. In 0.8 miles, turn left into parking lot. You have arrived at your destination.

Cathedral Park (nature)
N Pittsburg Avenue & N Edison Street, Portland, Oregon 97203
(503)823-7529
5:00 a.m.–12:00 a.m.
Free
From Salem, head north on I-5 toward Portland. In 40.0 miles, take exit 299B to merge onto I-405 North. In 0.3 miles, keep right on I-405 North. In 2.5 miles, take exit 3 to merge onto US-30 West. In 1.0 mile, continue onto NW Yeon Avenue. In 4.0 miles, take a slight left turn onto NW Bridge Avenue. In 0.5 miles, turn right onto NW Saint John's Historic Bridge. In 0.7 miles, turn right onto North Syracuse Street. In 200 feet, turn right onto North Burlington Avenue. In 700

feet, turn right onto North Salem Avenue. In 500 feet, turn right onto North Crawford Avenue. In 250 feet, turn left onto North Pittsburgh Avenue. In 200 feet, your destination will be on your right.

Boyd Cave (nature; hiking required)

Bend, Oregon 97702

24-7

Free

From Bend, head south on US-97. In 4.6 miles, take exit 143 onto Baker Road. In 0.3 miles, turn left onto Baker Road. In 1.4 miles, turn right onto China Hat Road. In 8.2 miles, prepare to park your vehicle near Coyote Loopa. Head left onto Coyote Loopa. In 0.25 miles, you will arrive at your destination.

Silver Falls State Park (nature)

20024 Silver Falls Highway SE, Silverton, Oregon 97385

(503)873-8681

8:00 a.m.–7:00 p.m.

$5

From Portland, head south on I-5 toward Salem. In 18.0 miles, take exit 282A onto OR-551 toward Canby. In 1.8 miles, turn left onto South Arndt Road NE. In 1.8 miles, turn right onto South Arndt Road. In 0.5 miles, turn right onto South Barlow Road. In 12.0 miles, turn left onto Meridian Road NE. In 4.1 miles, turn left onto Abiqua Road NE. In 0.9 miles, turn right onto Cascade Highway NE. In 0.9 miles, turn left onto Valley View Road NE. In 1.4 miles, turn right onto Evans Valley Road NE. In 500 feet, turn left onto Madrona Heights Drive NE. In 1.1 miles, turn right onto Quall Road NE. In 0.3 miles, turn right onto Forest Ridge Road NE. In 1.1 miles, keep right onto Silver Falls Drive NE. In 12.0 miles, turn left. In 600 feet, keep left. In 700 feet, keep left. In 350 feet, turn left. In 1.4 miles, your destination will be on your left.

Redmond Caves (nature)
3635 SW Airport Way, Redmond, Oregon 97756
Open 24 hours
Free
From Bend, head north on US-97 toward Redmond. In 14.0 miles, take exit 124 onto Airport Way toward Redmond Airport. In 0.2 miles, turn right onto SW Airport Way. In 1.1 miles, your destination will be on your left.

High Desert Museum (historical)
59800 S Highway 97, Bend, Oregon 97702
(541)382-4754
10:00 a.m.–4:00 p.m.
$15
From Portland, head south on I-5 toward Salem. In 9.5 miles, continue onto I-5 South. In 34.0 miles, take exit 253 to merge onto OR-22 toward Bend. In 0.3 miles, turn left to merge onto OR-22. In 13.0 miles, continue onto Santiam Highway. In 67.0 miles, continue onto Santiam Highway. In 25.0 miles, at the roundabout, take the second exit onto West Highway 20. In 21.0 miles, take a slight right turn onto US-97 South. In 8.0 miles, turn left. In 0.6 miles, you will arrive at your destination.

Portland Underground Tours (historical)

120 NW 3rd Avenue, Portland, Oregon 97209

(503)622-4798

Monday–Thursday 11:00 a.m.–9:30 p.m.; Friday–Saturday 11:00 a.m.–10:00 p.m.; Sunday 11:00 a.m.–6:30 p.m.

$15

From Salem, head north on I-5 toward Portland. In 34.0 miles, take exit 294 toward Barbur Boulevard. In 0.5 miles, continue ahead. In 5.4 miles, keep left onto South Barbur Boulevard. In 0.8 miles, turn left onto SW Caruthers Street. In 40 feet, keep right onto SW Broadway. In 700 feet, take a slight right turn onto SW 6th Avenue. In 200 feet, take a slight left turn to merge onto I-405 north. In 1.2 miles, take exit 2B. In 900 feet, turn right onto NW Everett Street. In 0.6 miles, turn right onto NW 3rd Avenue. In 350 feet, your destination will be on your left.

Wreck of the Peter Iredale (historical; best seen at low tide)

Peter Iredale Road, Astoria, Oregon 97103

(503)861-3170

6:00 a.m.–10:00 p.m.

$5

From Portland, head west on US-26 toward Beaverton. In 73.0 miles, take a slight right turn onto US-101 North toward Astoria. In 14.0 miles, turn left onto Highway 104. In 1.4 miles, turn left onto SW 18th Street. In 3.2 miles, turn left onto Peter Iredale Road. In 0.8 miles, turn left onto Peter Iredale Road. In 0.4 miles, prepare to park your vehicle, your destination will straight ahead.

Pittock Mansion Museum (historical)

3229 NW Pittock Drive, Portland, Oregon 97210

(503)823-3623

Thursday–Monday

$11

From Eugene, head north on I-5 toward Portland. In 98.0 miles, take exit 292A to merge onto OR-217 North toward Tigard. In 7.5 miles, take exit onto Barnes Road. In 700 feet, keep right onto Barnes Road East. In 3.2 miles, turn left onto NW Barnes Road. In 600 feet, turn right onto NW Pittock Avenue. In 900 feet, turn right onto NW Pittock Drive. In 0.3 miles, your destination will be on your left.

Timberline Lodge (historical)
10:00 a.m.–4:00 p.m.
27500 E Timberline Road, Government Camp, Oregon 97028
(503)272-3311
Open 24 hours
Free to look
From Bend, head north on US-97 toward Redmond. In 105.0 miles, turn right onto Timberline Highway. In 150 feet, turn right onto Timberline Highway. In 4.8 miles, continue onto east Timberline Road. You have arrived at your destination.

The Witches Castle (historical; hiking required)
Lower Macleay Trail, Portland, Oregon 97210
(503)823-4000
5:00 a.m.–10:00 p.m.
Free
From Salem, head north on I-5 toward Portland. In 32.0 miles, take exit 292A to merge onto OR-217 North toward Tigard. In 7.5 miles, take exit onto Barnes Road. In 700 feet, keep right onto Barnes Road East. In 1.4 miles, turn left onto SW Miller Road. In 2.1 miles, prepare to park your vehicle. Head sharp left. In 0.5 miles, you will arrive at your destination.

Allen Elizabethan Theatre (historical)
15 South Pioneer Street, Ashland, Oregon 97520
(800)219-8161
Show times vary
Ticket prices vary
From Eugene, head south on I-5. In 173.0 miles, take exit 19 toward Ashland. In 0.2 miles, turn right onto South Valley View Road. In 0.4 miles, turn left onto Highway 99 North. In 2.2 miles, turn right onto South Pioneer Street. In 250 feet, your destination will be on your right.

The Astoria Column (historical)
1 Coxcomb Drive, Astoria, Oregon 97013
(503)325-2963
10:00 a.m.–6:00 p.m.
$5
From Portland, head west on US-26 toward Beaverton. In 52.0 miles, turn left. In 600 feet, turn right onto OR-103. In 8.9 miles, turn left onto OR-202. In 26.0 miles, turn right onto Williamsport Road. In 1.1 miles, turn right onto 15th Street. In 350 feet, turn right onto Coxcomb Drive. In 0.7 miles, your destination will be on your left.

Vista House/Crown Point (historical)

40700 E Historic Columbia River Highway, Corbett, Oregon 97019

(503)344-1368

Monday–Friday 8:00 a.m.–5:00 p.m.

Donation

From Portland, head east on I-84 toward The Dalles. In 20.0 miles, take exit 22 toward Corbett. In 800 feet, turn right onto NE Corbett Hill Road. In 1.4 miles, turn left onto NE Corbett Hill Road. In 0.5 miles, keep left onto East Historic Columbia River Highway. In 1.4 miles, keep left onto East Historic Columbia River Highway. In 0.8 miles, you will arrive at your destination.

Dee Wright Observatory (historical)

Mckenzie Highway, Sisters, Oregon 97759

(800)832-1355

24-7 (closed during winter)

Free

From Bend, head north on US-97 toward Redmond. In 2.3 miles, take a slight right turn onto US-20 West toward Sisters. In 20.0 miles, turn left onto West Hood Avenue. In 0.2 miles, turn right onto McKenzie Highway. In 15.0 miles, prepare to park your vehicle. Head right onto Dee Wright. In 180 feet, turn right onto Dee Wright Observatory. In 40 feet, you will arrive at your destination.

Train Mountain Railroad Museum (historical)

36941 S Chiloquin Road, Chiloquin, Oregon 97624

(541)783-3030

Monday–Friday 9:00 a.m.–3:00 p.m.

$20

From Bend, head south on US-97. In 50.0 miles, keep left onto US-97. In 55.0 miles, your destination will be on your right.

Frank Lloyd Wright's Gordon House (historical)

879 W Main Street, Silverton, Oregon 97381

(503)874-6006

Wednesday–Sunday 12:00 p.m.–3:00 p.m.

$45

From Eugene, head north on I-5 toward Portland. In 57.0 miles, take exit 252 onto Kuebler Boulevard. In 0.4 miles, turn right onto Kuebler Boulevard SE. In 7.4 miles, turn right onto Silverton Road NE. In 7.4 miles, turn right onto Paradise Alley Road NE. In 1.0 mile, turn left onto West Main Street. In 0.2 miles, turn right. In 0.3 miles, turn right. In 250 feet, your destination will be on your right.

Erickson Collection Aircraft (historical)
2408 NW Berg Drive, Madras, Oregon 97741
(541)460-5065
Tuesday–Sunday 10:00 a.m.–5:00 p.m.
$9
From Bend, head north on US-97 toward Redmond. In 44.0 miles, turn left onto NW Cherry Lane. In 0.6 miles, turn right onto NW Berg Drive. In 0.4 miles, your destination will be on your left.

Evergreen Aviation and Space Museum and World's Largest Wooden Airplane (historical)
500 NE Captain Michael King Smith Way, McMinnville, Oregon 97128
(503)434-4180
10:00 a.m.–4:00 p.m.
$27+
From Salem, head west on OR-22. In 0.4 miles, keep left onto OR-22 West. In 9.2 miles, take exit 16 onto OR-99 West toward McMinnville. In 0.5 miles, turn left onto North Pacific Highway. In 18.0 miles, turn right onto OR-18 East. In 1.5 miles, keep left onto SW Highway 18. In 1.5 miles, turn left onto Cumulus Avenue. In 500 feet, turn right onto NE Cumulus Avenue. In 0.3 miles, continue onto NE Captain Michael King Smith Way. In 0.2 miles, you will arrive at your destination.

The USS *Blueback* (historical)
945 SE Water Avenue, Portland, Oregon 97214
(503)797-4000
Tuesday–Sunday 9:30 a.m.–5:30 p.m.
$8.50
From Salem, head north on I-5 toward Portland. In 40.0 miles, keep right on I-5 North. In 1.1 miles, take exit 300 to merge onto I-84 East. In 0.2 miles, take the exit onto SE Water Avenue. In 0.5 miles, turn right into the parking lot. You have arrived at your destination.

Baldwin Hotel Museum (historical)
31 Main Street, Klamath Falls, Oregon 97601
(541)883-4207
10:00 a.m.–4:00 p.m.
$10
From Bend, head South on US-97. In 50.0 miles, keep left onto Highway 97 North. In 76.0 miles, keep left onto Dalles-California Highway. In 1.4 miles, keep right to merge onto US-97 toward

Weed. In 2.4 miles, take exit toward Favell Museum. In 700 feet, turn right onto West Main Street toward City Center. In 800 feet, your destination will be on your left.

Yaquina Head Lighthouse (historical)

750 Lighthouse Drive, Unit 7, Newport, Oregon 97365

(541)574-3100

8:00 a.m.–6:00 p.m.

$7 (per car)

From Eugene, head north on I-5 toward Portland. In 34.0 miles, take exit 228 onto OR-34 toward Corvallis. In 0.3 miles, turn left onto Highway 34 SE toward Linn. In 9.8 miles, turn left onto OR-34. In 1.0 mile, continue onto Corvallis-Newport Highway. In 30.0 miles, continue ahead. In 4.5 miles, continue onto US-20. In 14 miles, turn right onto North Coast Highway. In 2.7 miles, turn left onto NW Lighthouse Drive. In 1.0 mile, your destination will be on your right.

Pete French Round Barn State Heritage Site (historical)

52229 Lava Bed Road, Diamond, Oregon 97722

(800)551-6949

Sunrise to sunset

Free

From Bend, head NW on Greenwood Avenue. In 130.0 miles, continue onto East Monroe Street. In 38.0 miles, keep right onto Lava Bed Road. In 1.2 miles, keep right onto Lava Bed Road. In 1.8 miles, keep left onto Lava Bed Road. In 11.0 miles, turn left onto Round Bar. In 0.9 miles, you will arrive at your destination.

Tamástslikt Cultural Museum (archaeological)

47106 Wildhorse Boulevard, Pendleton, Oregon 97801

(541)429-7700

Monday–Saturday 10:00 a.m.–5:00 p.m.

From Portland, head east on I-84 toward The Dalles. In 213.0 miles, take exit 216 toward Walla Walla. In 0.3 miles, turn left onto OR-331 toward Mission. In 0.9 miles, turn right onto Wildhorse Boulevard. In 0.5 miles, you will arrive at your destination.

Idaho

Oasis Bordello Museum (obscure)
605 Cedar Street, Wallace, Idaho 83873
(208)753-0801
10:00 a.m.–5:00 p.m.
$5
From Coeur d'Alene, head east on I-90 toward Kellogg. In 46.0 miles, take exit 61 onto I-90 BL toward Wallace. In 0.2 miles, turn right toward South Frontage Road. In 450 feet, turn left onto Front Street. In 0.5 miles, turn left on Cedar Street. In 500 feet, your destination will be on your left.

North Idaho Trading Company & Antiques (obscure)
504 Banks Street, Wallace, Idaho 83878
(208)753-2911
Monday–Saturday 9:00 a.m.–5:00 p.m.
Free to look
From Coeur d'Alene, head east on I-90 toward Kellogg. In 46.0 miles, take exit 61 onto I-90 BL toward Wallace. In 0.2 miles, turn right toward South Frontage Road. In 450 feet, turn left onto Front Street. In 0.6 miles, turn left onto Bank Street. Your destination will be on your right.

Dog Park Inn/World's Largest Beagle (obscure)
2421 Business Loop 95, Cottonwood, Idaho 83522
(208)962-3647
Studio 11:00 a.m.–4:00 p.m.; lodging April–October
Free to look
From Boise, head west on I-84. In 46.0 miles, take exit 3 onto US-95 toward Fruitland. In 0.2 miles, turn right onto US-95. In 6.0 miles, keep right onto South 16th Street. In 45.0 miles, turn right onto East Central Boulevard. In 47.0 miles, turn left onto North Norris Avenue. In 76.0 miles, turn left onto Johnston Road. In 2.2 miles, turn left onto Highway 95 North. In 13.0 miles, turn left onto Bus US-95. In 0.3 miles, turn left. Your destination will be on your left.

Spud Drive-In (obscure)

2175 South Highway 33, Driggs, Idaho 83422

(208)352-2727

Thursday–Saturday 6:30 p.m.–10:30 p.m.

$9.50

From Pocatello, head north on I-15 toward Twin Falls. In 48.0 miles, take exit 119 to merge onto US-20 East toward Rigby. In 31.0 miles, take exit 339 toward Driggs. In 0.4 miles, turn right onto East Ninth North. In 44.0 miles, turn left. You have arrived at your destination.

Dugout Dick Memorial/Idaho Hermits Historical Marker (obscure)

Loening Road off US Highway 93 Salmon, Idaho 83467

Daily

Free

From Idaho Falls, take I-15 north toward Roberts. In 24.0 miles, take exit 143 onto SH-33 toward Salmon. In 0.2 miles, turn left onto East 1500 North INL site. In 15.0 miles, stay right onto Salmon Highway. In 120.0 miles, turn left onto South Challis Street. In 19.0 miles, turn right. In 300 feet, turn left onto Loening Road. In 0.5 miles, you will arrive at your destination.

Cleo's Ferry Museum and Nature Trail (obscure)

1984 Highway 45, Melba, Idaho 83641

(208)495-2688

8:00 a.m.–7:00 p.m.

From Boise, head west on I-84. In 13.0 miles, take exit 36 onto North Franklin Boulevard. In 0.2 miles, turn left onto North Franklin Boulevard toward City Center. In 0.9 miles, turn right onto 11th Avenue North. In 0.8 miles, turn left onto Third Street South. In 400 feet, turn right onto 12th Avenue South. In 17.0 miles, take a slight left turn. You have arrived at your destination.

Perrine Memorial Bridge (obscure)

3591 N 3000 E, Twin Falls, Idaho 83301

(208)733-9458

24-7

$5

From Boise, head east on I-84 toward Mountain Home. In 123.0 miles, take exit 173 onto US-93 toward Twin Falls. In 0.8 miles, keep right onto US-93 South. In 2.7 miles, your destination will be on your right.

Idaho Potato Museum and Potato Station Café (obscure)

130 NW Main Street, Blackfoot, Idaho 83221

(208)785-2517

9:30 a.m.–5:00 p.m.

$6

From Pocatello, head north on I-15 toward Blackfoot. In 18.0 miles, take exit 89 onto I-15 BL toward Blackfoot. In 0.3 miles, turn left onto I-15 BL. In 3.3 miles, continue onto NW Main Street. In 450 feet, your destination will be on your right.

Discovery Center of Idaho (obscure)

131 W Myrtle Street, Boise, Idaho 83702

(208)343-9895

Monday–Saturday 10:00 a.m.–4:30 p.m.; Sunday 12:00 p.m.–4:30 p.m.

$18

From Twin Falls, head west on I-84. In 119.0 miles, take exit 54 onto US-20. In 0.3 miles, turn right onto South Broadway Avenue. In 2.9 miles, turn left onto East Front Street. In 0.3 miles, turn left onto South Second Street. In 500 feet, turn left onto West Myrtle Street. In 150 feet, your destination will be on your right.

Center of The Universe (obscure)

414 6th Street, Wallace, Idaho 83873

24-7

Free

From Coeur d'Alene, head east onto I-90 toward Kellogg. In 47.0 miles, take exit 62 toward Wallace. In 0.3 miles, turn right onto Bank Street. In 0.4 miles, you will arrive at your destination.

Museum of Clean (obscure)

711 S 2nd Avenue, Pocatello, Idaho

(208)236-6906

Tuesday–Saturday 10:00 a.m.–5:00 p.m.

$6

From Twin Falls, head east on I-84 toward Pocatello. In 39.0 miles, continue onto I-86 East. In 58.0 miles, take exit 58 onto US-30 toward West Pocatello. In 0.4 miles, turn right onto US-30. In 4.4 miles, turn left onto East Gould Street. In 0.4 miles, turn right onto Pocatello Avenue. In 1.1 miles, turn right onto East Benton Avenue. In 700 feet, turn left onto South Second Avenue. In 800 feet, turn right into the parking lot. Your destination will be on your left.

Spur Sculpture by John Grade (obscure) (hiking required)
Wood River Trails, Ketchum, Idaho 83340
(208)726-9491
24-7
Free
From Boise, head east on I-84. In 40.0 miles, take exit 95 onto US-20 toward Fairfield. In 0.3 miles, turn left onto US-20 toward Sun Valley. In 82.0 miles, turn left onto SH-75. In 26.0 miles, turn left onto Serenade Lane. In 900 feet, turn left onto Third Avenue. In 500 feet, prepare to park your vehicle near Wood River Trail. Take a left onto Wood River Trail. In 460 feet, walk over the bridge. In 0.2 miles, your destination will be on your left.

Shoshone Ice Cavern (nature; hiking required)
1561 Scenic Highway 75 N, Shoshone, Idaho 833352
(208)886-2058
$10
10:00 a.m.–6:00 p.m.
From Twin Falls, head west on I-84. In 86.0 miles, take exit 141 toward US-26. In 0.3 miles, turn left onto US-26. In 27.0 miles, turn left onto South Greenwood Street. In 200 feet, continue onto North Greenwood Street. In 16.0 miles, turn left onto Ice Cave Road. In 0.3 miles, you will arrive at your destination.

The Black Cliffs (nature)
9800 East Highway 21, Boise, Idaho 83716
24-7
Free
From Twin Falls, head east on I-84. In 116.0 miles, take exit 57 onto SH-21. In 0.2 miles, turn right onto East Gowen Road toward Idaho City. In 13.0 miles, turn right onto East Spring Shores Road. In 1.4 miles, turn right onto Deer Creek Road. In 200 feet, make a U-turn. In 200 feet, turn left onto Arrow Rock Road. In 1.4 miles, turn left onto East Highway 21. In 8.6 miles, your destination will be on your right.

Shoshone Falls Park (nature)
4186 Shoshone Falls Grade Road, Twin Falls, Idaho 83301
(208)736-22656
7:30 a.m.–6:12 p.m.
$5

From Boise, head east on I-84. In 119.0 miles, take exit 173 onto US-93 toward Twin Falls. In 0.8 miles, keep right onto US-93 South. In 2.9 miles, turn left onto Bridgeview Boulevard. In 0.4 miles, turn left onto Pole Line Road East. In 1.5 miles, turn left onto Falls Avenue East. In 2.0 miles, turn left onto North 3300 East. In 0.9 miles, keep right onto Shoshone Falls Grade Road. In 0.5 miles, you will arrive at your destination.

Craters of the Moon (nature; hiking required)
1266 Craters Loop Road, Arco, Idaho 82313
(208)527-1300
7th Street
$10
From Boise, head east on I-84 toward Mountain Home. In 40.0 miles, take exit 95 onto US-20 toward Fairfield. In 0.3 miles, turn left onto US-20. In 100.0 miles, turn left onto North Main Street. In 25.0 miles, turn right onto Loop Road. Your destination will be on your left.

Custer Ghost Town (historical)
Yankee Fork Road, Challis, Idaho 83226
Daily
Free to look
From Boise, head east on I-84. In 40.0 miles, take exit 95 onto US-20 toward Fairfield. In 0.3 miles, turn left onto US-20. In 82.0 miles, turn left onto SH-75. In 100.0 miles, turn left onto Yankee Fork Road. In 9.9 miles, you will arrive at your destination.

Kuna Caves (nature) (hiking required)
Kuna Cave Road, Kuna, Idaho 83634
(206)922-5546
24-7
Free
From Boise, head west on I-84. In 4.6 miles, take exit 44 onto SH-69 South toward Kuna. In 0.3 miles, stay left to turn onto South Meridian Road. In 8.2 miles, turn left onto Swan Falls Road. In 4.6 miles, turn right onto West Kuna Cave Road. In 2.0 miles, turn left onto Black Cat Road. In 0.7 miles, go through cattle guard (close behind you). In 1,700 feet, you will arrive at your destination.

Geyser Park (nature)
76 South Main Street, Soda Springs, Idaho 83276
(208)547-4964
Daily
Free to look
From Pocatello, head east on US-30. In 20.0 miles, take exit 47 onto US-30 East toward Soda Springs. In 0.3 miles, turn left onto US-30 toward McCammon. In 0.7 miles, continue onto East Highway 30. In 33.0 miles, turn left onto South Main Street. In 800 feet, turn left onto First Street South. In 350 feet, your destination will be on your right.

Jump Creek Falls (nature)
South Jump Creek Road, Marsing, Idaho 83639
(208)896-5912
6:00 a.m.–9:00 p.m.
Free
From Boise, head west on I-84 toward Nampa. In 15.0 miles, take exit 33A onto SH-55 South toward Nampa. In 0.3 miles, turn right onto West Karcher Road. In 17.0 miles, turn left onto US-95. In 2.5 miles, turn right onto Poison Creek Road. In 3.3 miles, turn left onto South Jump Creek Road. In 1.5 miles, stay right. In 0.3 miles, turn right. Your destination will be on your right.

City of Rocks National Reserve (nature; hiking required)
3035 South Elba-Almo Road, Almo, Idaho 83312
(208) 824-5901
8:00 a.m.–4:30 p.m.
Free
From Twin Falls, head east on I-84 toward Burley. In 34.0 miles, take exit 216 onto SH-77 toward Declo. In 0.2 miles, turn right onto North Highway 77 toward Delco. In 12.0 miles, turn right onto South Main Street. In 0.4 miles, stay left onto South Highway 77. In 11.0 miles, turn right onto South Elba-Almo Road. In 17.0 miles, turn right onto 3075 South. In 4.1 miles, take a slight right turn onto City of Rocks Road. In 0.5 miles, your destination will be on your left.

Hagerman Fossil Beds (nature)
221 N State Street, Hagerman, Idaho 83332
(208)933-4105
Friday–Sunday 10:00 a.m.–4:30 p.m.
Free
From Boise, head east on I-84. In 86.0 miles, take exit 141 toward Hagerman. In 0.3 miles, turn right toward US-30. In 900 feet, turn left onto US-30. In 13.0 miles, turn right onto Bell Rapids Road. In 6.5 miles, take a slight right turn onto North 400 East. In 2.0 miles, turn right. In 200 feet, you will arrive at your destination.

Upper Mesa Falls (nature; closed during winter; hiking required)
Upper Mesa Falls Road, Saint Anthony, Idaho 83445
(208)652-7442
Summer 9:30 a.m.–5:30 p.m.
$5
From Pocatello, head north on I-15 toward Blackfoot. In 48.0 miles, take exit 119 to merge onto US-20 East toward Rigby. In 0.2 miles, turn right to merge onto US-20 east. In 4.8 miles, keep left onto Mesa Falls Scenic Byway. In 10.0 miles, turn left onto Upper Mesa Falls Road. In 0.8 miles, your destination will be on your right.

Idaho Botanical Gardens (nature)
2355 N Old Penitentiary Road, Boise, Idaho 83712
(208)343-8649
Monday–Friday 9:00 a.m.–5:00 p.m.
$8

From Twin Falls, head west on I-84 toward Boise. In 119.0 miles, take exit 54 onto US-20. In 0.3 miles, turn right onto South Broadway Avenue. In 2.9 miles, continue onto South Broadway Avenue. In 0.2 miles, turn right onto East Warm Springs Avenue. In 1.5 miles, turn left onto East Goodman Street. In 0.2 miles, turn left. In 200 feet, turn right onto East Old Penitentiary. In 450 feet, your destination will be on your left.

Minnetonka Cave (nature)
Minnetonka Cave Road, Saint Charles, Idaho 83272
(435)245-4422
10:00 a.m.–5:30 p.m.
$4
From Pocatello, head south on I-15 toward McCammon. In 22.0 miles, take exit 47 onto US-30 East toward Soda Springs. In 0.3 miles, turn left onto US-30 toward Lava Hot Springs. In 0.7 miles, continue onto East Highway 30. In 63.0 miles, turn right onto Washington Street. In 0.7 miles, keep left onto Washington Street. In 5.1 miles, keep left onto US-89. In 11.0 miles, turn right onto Minnetonka Cave Road. In 10.0 miles, you will arrive at your destination.

Lava Hot Springs (nature)
430 E Main Street, Lava Hot Springs, Idaho 83246
(208)776-5221
Sunday–Thursday 9:00 a.m.–10:00 p.m.; Friday–Saturday 9:00 a.m.–11:00 p.m.
$6
From Pocatello, head east on US-30. In 20.0 miles, take exit 47 onto US-30 East toward Soda Springs. In 0.3 miles, turn left onto US-30 toward Lava Hot Springs. In 0.7 miles, continue onto East Highway 30. In 12.0 miles, turn right onto East Main Street. In 600 feet, your destination will be on your right.

Gold Fork Hot Springs (nature; cash only)
1026 Gold Fork Road, McCall, Idaho 83638
(208)890-8730
Sunday–Friday 12:00 p.m.–9:00 p.m.; Saturday 12:00 p.m.–11:00 p.m.
$8
From Boise, head north on SH-55. In 83.0 miles, turn right onto Davis Creek Lane. In 2.5 miles, turn right onto Gold Fork Road. In 2.4 miles, turn right onto Gold Fork Road. In 1.7 miles, turn left. Your destination will be on your left.

Nez Perce National Historic Park/Heart of the Monster (nature)

Hemo Trail, Kamiah, Idaho 83536

Sunrise to sunset

Free

From Coeur d' Alene, head south on US-95. In 83.0 miles, turn right onto South Main Street. In 29.0 miles, keep left onto US-95 South toward Boise. In 7.6 miles, continue onto US-95 South. In 1.9 miles, turn left. Your destination will be on your right.

Sierra Silver Mine Tour (nature)

509 Cedar Street, Wallace, Idaho 83873

(208)752-5151

10:00 a.m.–4:00 p.m.

$16

From Coeur d'Alene, head east on I-90 toward Kellogg. In 46.0 miles, take exit 61 onto I-90 BL toward Wallace. In 0.2 miles, turn right toward Wallace. In 450 feet, turn left onto Front Street. In 0.5 miles, turn left onto Cedar Street. In 150 feet, your destination will be on your left.

Idaho's Mammoth Cave (nature)

251 Thorn Creek Road, Shoshone, Idaho 83352

(208)539-7072

9:00 a.m.–6:00 p.m.

$10

From Boise, head east on I-84. In 86.0 miles, take exit 141 toward Gooding. In 0.3 miles, turn left onto US-26. In 27.0 miles, turn left onto South Greenwood Street. In 200 feet, continue onto North Greenwood Street. In 8.4 miles, turn left onto Mammoth Cave Civil Defense Road. In 1.2 miles, turn left. In 0.4 miles, your destination will be on your right.

Kathryn Albertson Park (nature)

1001 N Americana Boulevard, Boise, Idaho 83706

(208)608-7644

6:00 a.m.–8:00 p.m.

Free

From Twin Falls, head east on I-84. In 120.0 miles, take exit 53 onto Vista Avenue toward Boise Airport. In 0.2 miles, turn right onto South Vista Avenue. In 1.2 miles, turn left onto West Overland Road. In 0.7 miles, turn right onto South Latah Street. In 1.5 miles, turn right onto South American Boulevard. In 0.3 miles, turn left onto Albertson Park. You have arrived at your destination.

Thousand Springs State Park (nature)
2314 Ritchie Road, Hangerman, Idaho 83332
(208)837-4505
Monday–Friday 7:30 a.m.–4:00 p.m.
$5
From Boise, head east on I-84. In 93.0 miles, take exit toward Tuttle. In 0.3 miles, turn right onto East 2350 South toward Hangerman. In 0.3 miles, turn right onto Ritchie Road. In 0.3 miles, turn left. In 0.3 miles, turn left. In 600 feet, your destination will be on your left.

Idaho Museum of Natural History (nature)
698 E Dillon Street, Pocatello, Idaho 83209
(208)282-3168
Tuesday–Friday, Sunday 12:00 p.m.–5:00 p.m.; Saturday 10:00 a.m.–5:00 p.m.
$7
From Boise, head east on I-84. In 167.0 miles, continue onto I-86 East. In 63.0 miles, take exit 63A to merge onto I-15 South toward Salt Lake. In 2.4 miles, take exit 69 onto Clark Street. In 0.4 miles, keep right toward Historic Old Town. In 0.5 miles, turn left onto North 15th Avenue. In 0.7 miles, turn right onto Martin Luther King Jr. Way. In 0.2 miles, turn left onto South Eighth Avenue. In 0.2 miles, turn right onto East Humboldt Street. In 300 feet, turn right into the parking lot. You have arrived at your destination.

Burke Ghost Town (historical)
Burke Canyon Creek Road, Wallace, Idaho
Daily
Free
From Coeur d'Alene, head east on I-90. In 47.0 miles, take exit 62 toward Burke. In 0.3 miles, turn left onto Bank Street. In 6.3 miles, turn right onto Shifters Hill. You have arrived at your destination.

Warhawk Air Museum (historical)
201 Municipal Drive, Nampa, Idaho 83687
(208)465-6446
Tuesday–Saturday 10:00 a.m.–5:00 p.m.; Sunday 11:00 a.m.–4:00 p.m.
$12
From Boise, head west on I-84 toward Nampa. In 11.0 miles, take exit 38 onto Garrity Boulevard. In 0.3 miles, turn left onto Garrity Boulevard toward Nampa. In 0.8 miles, turn left onto North 39th Street. In 0.4 miles, your destination will be on your right.

Minidoka National Historic Site (historical)
Hunt Road, Jerome, Idaho 83338
(208)825-4169
8:00 a.m.–9:00 p.m.
Free
From Boise, head east on I-84 toward Mountain Home. In 110.0 miles, take exit 165 onto SH-25 toward Jerome. In 0.2 miles, turn left on SH-25. In 15.0 miles, take a slight left turn onto East 400 South. In 0.3 miles, turn left onto Hunt Road. In 2.5 miles, your destination will be on your right.

Idaho Black History Museum (historical)
508 Julia Davis Drive, Boise, Idaho 83702
(208)789-2164
Tuesday–Thursday 10:00 a.m.–3:00 p.m.; Saturday 11:00 a.m.–3:00 p.m.
Free
From Twin Falls, head west on I-84. In 120.0 miles, take exit 53 onto Vista Avenue. In 0.2 miles, turn right onto South Vista Avenue. In 2.1 miles, turn left onto South Capitol Boulevard. In 0.7 miles, turn right onto South Capitol Boulevard. In 800 feet, your destination will be on your left.

Map Rock (historical)
Melba, Idaho 83641
Daily
Free
From Boise, head west on I-84 toward Nampa. In 13.0 miles, take exit 36 onto North Franklin Boulevard. In 0.2 miles, turn left onto North Franklin Boulevard toward City Center. In 0.9 miles, turn right onto 11th Avenue North. In 0.8 miles, turn left onto Third Street South. In 400 feet, turn right onto 12th Avenue South. In 11.0 miles, turn right onto Melmont Road. In 5.0 miles, turn left onto Pump Road. In 1.4 miles, turn right onto Map Rock Road. In 2.5 miles, your destination will be on your right.

Old Idaho Penitentiary (historical)
2445 Old Penitentiary Road, Boise, Idaho 83712
(208)334-2844
Tuesday–Sunday 12:00 p.m.–5:00 p.m.
$6
From Twin Falls, head east on I-84. In 119.0 miles, take exit 54 onto US-20. In 0.3 miles, turn right onto South Broadway Avenue. In 2.9 miles, continue onto South Broadway Avenue.

In 0.2 miles, turn right onto East Warm Springs Avenue. In 1.4 miles, turn left onto East Old Penitentiary Road. In 0.4 miles, your destination will be on your right.

Treaty Rock (historical)
302 West Seltice Way, Post Falls, Idaho 83854
(208)773-0539
Sunrise to sunset
Free
From Coeur d'Alene, head west on I-90 toward Spokane. In 8.6 miles, take exit 5 onto Spokane Street. In 0.3 miles, turn right onto North Spokane Street toward I-90 BL. In 350 feet, turn left onto West Seventh Avenue. In 600 feet, turn right onto North Compton Street. In 300 feet, turn left. Your destination will be in your right.

Birch Creek Charcoal Kilns (historical)
Forest Service Road 541, Salmon, Idaho 83467
Daily
Free
From Idaho Falls, take I-15 north toward Roberts. In 24.0 miles, take exit 143 onto SH-133 toward Salmon. In 0.2 miles, turn left onto East 1500 North toward INL Site. In 15.0 miles, stay right onto North Salmon Highway. In 46.0 miles, turn left onto Forest Service Road 188. Turn left onto Forest Service Road 188. In 5.2 miles, you will arrive at your destination.

Basque Museum and Culture Center (historical)
611 W Grove Street, Boise, Idaho 83702
(208)343-2671
Tuesday–Friday 10:00 a.m.–5:00 p.m.; Saturday 11:00 a.m.–4:00 p.m.
$5
From Twin Falls, head west on I-84 toward Boise. In 119.0 miles, take exit 54 onto US-20. In 0.3 miles, turn right onto S Broadway Avenue. In 2.9 miles, turn left onto East Front Street. In 0.5 miles, turn right onto East Front Street. In 400 feet, turn left onto West Grove Street. In 500 feet, your destination will be on your left.

Ernest Hemingway's Grave (historical)

1026 N Main Street, Ketchum, Idaho 83340

(208)726-9201

Dawn to dusk

Free

From Boise, head east on I-84. In 40.0 miles, take exit 95 onto US-20 toward Fairfield. In 0.3 miles, turn left onto US-20. In 82.0 miles, turn left onto SH-75. In 27.0 miles, your destination will be on your right.

Celebration Park and Petroglyphs (archaeological)

6530 Hot Spot Lane, Melba, Idaho 83641

(208)455-6022

10:00 a.m.–2:00 p.m.

$2

From Boise, head west on I-84 toward Nampa. In 4.6 miles, take exit 44 onto SH-69 South toward Meridian. In 0.3 miles, take a slight left turn onto South Meridian Road. In 8.2 miles, turn left onto Swan Falls Road. In 4.0 miles, turn left onto South Robinson Boulevard. In 0.8 miles, keep right onto West Dickman Road. In 1.1 miles, turn left onto South Can Ada Road. In 2.5 miles, turn left onto South Can Ada Road. In 300 feet, turn right onto South Can Ada Road. In 3.0 miles, turn right onto Warren Spur Road. In 1.6 miles, turn left onto Sinker Road. In 2.8 miles, turn left onto Hot Spot Lane. In 0.3 miles, your destination will be on your right.

Appaloosa Museum & Heritage Center (archaeological)

2720 Pullman Road, Moscow, Idaho 83843

(208)882-5578

Monday–Thursday 9:00 a.m.–1:30 p.m.; Friday 9:00 a.m.–1:30 p.m.; Saturday 11:00 a.m.–3:00 p.m.

Free

From Coeur d'Alene, head south on US-95 toward Moscow. In 83.0 miles, turn right onto West Third Street. In 0.2 miles, continue onto West Pullman Street. In 1.6 miles, turn right. In 200 feet, your destination will be on your left.

Montana

Ewam Garden of One Thousand Buddhas (obscure)
34574 White Coyote Road, Arlee, Montana 59821
(406)726-0555
9:00 a.m.–7:00 p.m.
Donation
From Missoula, head west on I-90. In 8.2 miles, take exit 96 on US-93 North, MT-200 West toward Kalispell. In 0.2 miles, stay right onto US-93 North. In 19.0 miles, turn right onto White Coyote Road. In 0.5 miles, turn left. In 100 feet, turn right. In 70 feet, prepare to park your vehicle.

Polebridge Mercantile Bakery (obscure)

265 Polebridge Loop, Polebridge, Montana 59928

(406)888-5105

Check website for hours

Free to look

From Missoula, head west on I-90. In 8.2 miles, take exit 96 onto US-93 North toward Kalispell. In 0.2 miles, keep right onto US-93 North. In 58.0 miles, turn right onto MT-35. In 45.0 miles, turn right onto S-206. In 9.7 miles, turn left onto US Highway 2 East. In 1.6 miles, turn right onto Nucleus Avenue. In 0.6 miles, turn right onto Railroad Street East. In 35.0 miles, turn right onto Polebridge Loop. In 150 feet, turn right onto Polebridge Loop. In 0.3 miles, your destination will be on your right.

The Sip 'n Dip Lounge (obscure)

17 7th Street South, Great Falls, Montana

(406)454-2141

Monday–Saturday 11:00 a.m.–2:00 a.m.; Sunday 12:00 p.m.–12:00 a.m.

Free to look

From Butte, head north on I-15. In 2.7 miles, take exit 129 to merge onto I-15 North toward Helena. In 45.0 miles, stay right on I-15 N. In 103.0 miles, take exit 278 onto I-15 BL, US-89 South toward 10th Avenue South. In 2.5 miles, turn left onto Sixth Street South. In 0.6 miles, turn right onto Second Avenue South. In 450 feet, turn left onto Seventh Street South. In 500 feet, your destination will be on your right.

American Computer and Robotics Museum (obscure)

2023 Stadium Drive, Bozeman, Montana 59715

(406)582-1288

Tuesday–Sunday 12:00 p.m.–4:00 p.m.

Donation

From Butte, head east on I-90. In 78.0 miles, take exit 305 onto North 19th Avenue. In 0.5 miles, turn right onto North 19th Avenue. In 3.7 miles, turn left onto Kagy Boulevard. In 0.4 miles, turn right onto Stadium Drive. In 700 feet, turn left. Your destination will be on your left.

Miracle of America Museum (obscure)

36094 Memory Lane, Polson, Montana 59860

(406)883-6804

9:00 a.m.–5:00 p.m.

$10

From Missoula, head west on I-90. In 8.2 miles, take exit 96 onto US-93 North toward Kalispell. In 0.2 miles, keep right onto US-93 North. In 58.0 miles, turn right onto Memory Lane. In 150 feet, turn left onto Memory Lane. In 500 feet, turn right. In 100 feet, turn right. Your destination will be on your left.

Blackfoot Pathways: Sculpture in the Wild (obscure)

1970 East MT-200, Lincoln, Montana 59639
Dawn to dusk
Free
From Butte, head north on I-15. In 2.7 miles, take exit 129 to merge onto I-15 North toward Helena. In 45.0 miles, keep right on I-15 North. In 25.0 miles, take exit 200 onto S-279. In 0.2 miles, turn left onto Lincoln Road East. In 2.5 miles, at the roundabout, take the second exit onto Lincoln Road West. In 36.0 miles, turn left onto MT-200. In 11.0 miles, turn right onto Sucker Creek Road. In 0.4 miles, turn right. In 0.2 miles, prepare to park your vehicle.

Montana Vortex and House of Mystery (obscure)

7800 US-2 E, Columbia Falls, Montana 59912
(406)892-1210
Open May 23rd–Labor Day Wednesday–Monday 10:00 a.m.–5:00 p.m. (closed Tuesday)
$12
From Missoula, head west on I-90. In 8.2 miles, take exit 96 onto US-93 North toward Kalispell. In 0.2 miles, keep right onto US-93 North. In 58.0 miles, turn right onto MT-35. In 45.0 miles, turn right onto S-206. In 9.7 miles, turn right onto US Highway 2 East. In 1.8 miles, turn left. Your destination will be on your left.

Tippet Rise Art Center (obscure)

96 S Grove Creek Road, Fishtail, Montana 59028
Friday–Sunday 10:00 a.m.–3:00 p.m.
$10
From Billings, head west on I-90 toward Butte. In 41.0 miles, take exit 408 onto MT-78 toward Columbus. In 0.3 miles turn left onto MT-78 toward Columbus. In 0.9 miles, turn right onto East Pike Avenue. In 0.2 miles, turn left onto South Pratten Street. In 17.0 miles, turn right onto South Pratten Street. In 3.4 miles, turn right onto West Main Street. In 0.5 miles, turn right onto Grove Creek Road. In 1.5 miles, turn right. In 300 feet, your destination will be on your left.

Kootenai Swinging Bridge (obscure; hiking required)

21311 US-2, Troy, Montana 59935

Daily

Free

From Missoula, head west on I-90. In 8.2 miles, take exit 96 onto MT-200 West. In 0.2 miles, keep right onto MT-200 West toward Kalispell. In 27.0 miles, turn left onto MT-200. In 105.0 miles, turn right onto Bull River Road. In 35.0 miles, turn right onto US-2. In 4.1 miles, your destination will be on your left.

Historic Dumas Brothel Museum (obscure)

45 E. Mercury Street, Butte, Montana

(406)530-7878

Saturday 10:00 a.m.–6:00 p.m.; Sunday 10:00 a.m.–1:00 p.m.

$10

From Missoula, head east on I-90. In 116.0 miles, take exit 124 to merge onto I-115 East toward City Center. In 1.4 miles, continue onto West Iron Street. In 0.3 miles, turn left onto South Montana Street. In 0.5 miles, turn right onto West Mercury Street. In 0.3 miles, your destination will be on your left.

Medicine Rocks State Park (nature)
1141 MT-7, Ekalaka, Montana 59324
(406)377-6256
7:00 a.m.–10:00 p.m.
Free
From Billings, head east on I-94 toward Bismark. In 140.0 miles, take exit 141 onto US-12 East toward Miles City. In 0.2 miles, turn right onto US-12. In 76.0 miles, turn right onto Main Street South. In 24.0 miles, turn right onto Park Entrance Road. Your destination will be on your right.

Lewis and Clark Caverns (nature)
25 Lewis and Clark Caverns Road, Whitehall, Montana 59759
(406)287-3541
May–September 9:00 a.m.–4:30 p.m.; Off-season 10:00 a.m.–4:00 p.m.
$12
From Butte, head east on I-90 toward Billings. In 29.0 miles, take exit 256 toward Cardwell. In 0.3 miles, turn right onto MT State Highway 2 East toward Cardwell. In 150 feet, turn left onto MT State Highway 2 East. In 7.4 miles, turn left. In 60 feet, your destination will be on your left.

Mysterious Ringing Rocks (nature; bring hammer and bear mace; high-clearance vehicle only; hiking required)
Whitehall, Montana 59759
Daily
Free
From Butte, head east on I-90 toward Billings. In 15.0 miles, take exit 241 toward Pipestone. In 900 feet, turn left onto Delmoe Lake Road. In 700 feet, turn right. In 1.2 miles, prepare to park your vehicle. Head right. In 0.25 miles, take a slight left. In 0.7 miles, take a slight right turn. In 2.2 miles, take a slight right turn. In 0.25 miles, your destination will be on your left.

Makoshika State Park (nature)
1301 Snyder Avenue, Glendive, Montana 59330
(406)377-6256
9:00 a.m.–5:00 p.m.
$9
From Billings, head east on I-94 toward Bismarck. In 209.0 miles, take exit 210 onto I-94 BL toward Glendive. In 3.6 miles, turn right onto North Douglas Street. In 0.8 miles, turn right onto South Taylor Avenue. In 0.4 miles, turn left onto Snyder Avenue. In 0.4 miles, you will arrive at your destination.

Glacier National Park (nature)
64 Grinnell Drive, West Glacier, Montana 59936
(406)888-7800
Open 24 hours
Summer $35; Winter $25
From Missoula, head west on I-90. In 8.2 miles, take exit 96 onto US-93 North toward Kalispell. In 0.2 miles, keep right onto US-93 North. In 58.0 miles, turn right onto MT-35. In 45.0 miles, turn right onto S-206. In 9.7 miles, turn right onto US Highway 2 East. In 15.0 miles, turn left onto Glacier Route One Road. In 100 feet, your destination will be on your right.

Going-to-the-Sun Road (nature)

Going-to-the-Sun Road, Essex, Montana 59916 (located inside of Glacier National Park)

Open usually late June or early July; closes 3rd Monday in October (weather permitting; closed during winter)

Free

From Missoula, head west on I-90. In 8.2 miles, take exit 96 onto US-93 North toward Kalispell. In 0.2 miles, keep right onto US-93 North. In 58.0 miles, turn right onto MT-35. In 45.0 miles, turn right onto S-206. In 9.7 miles, turn right onto US Highway 2 East. In 15.0 miles, turn left onto Glacier Route One Road. In 1.4 miles, you will arrive at your destination.

Our Lady of the Rockies (historical)

3100 Harrison Avenue, Butte, Montana 59701

(406)-782-1221

Can view year-round from road; tours are available June–October

Free to look; tour costs $18

From Butte, take I-15 north. Take exit 129 on the right to merge onto I-15 North toward Helena. In 4.8 miles, take exit 134 toward Woodville. In 0.2 miles, turn right. In 150 feet, turn right. In 4.9 miles, turn right. In 1.6 miles, turn left. In 500 feet, your destination will be on your right.

Bannack Ghost Town (historical)
4200 Bannack Road, Dillon, Montana
(406)834-3413
10:00 a.m.–6:00 p.m.
Free
From Butte, head south on I-15. In 2.7 miles, take exit 121 to merge onto I-15 South toward Dillon. In 62.0 miles, take exit 59 onto S-278 toward Jackson. In 0.3 miles, turn right onto S-278. In 17.0 miles, turn left onto Bannack Bench Road. In 2.9 miles, turn left onto Bannack Road. In 0.6 miles, turn right. You have arrived at your destination.

Castle Town (historical)
Forest Service Road 581, Martinsdale, Montana 59053
Daily
Free
From Butte, head north on I-15 toward Helena. In 2.7 miles, take exit 29 to merge onto I-15 North. In 45.0 miles, keep right on I-15 North. In 12.0 miles, take exit 187 onto S-518 toward Montana City. In 0.2 miles, turn right onto S-518. In 4.4 miles, turn right onto East US Highway 12. In 28.0 miles, turn left onto Broadway Street. In 33.0 miles, turn right onto US-89. In 7.9 miles, turn left onto S-294. In 16.0 miles, turn left onto Lennep Road. In 0.2 miles, take a sharp left turn onto Castle Town Road. In 7.3 miles, you will arrive at your destination.

Elkhorn Ghost Town (historical; four-wheel drive recommended)
811 Elkhorn Road, Boulder, Montana 59632
Daily
Free
From Butte, head north on I-15. In 2.7 miles, take exit 129 to merge onto I-15 North toward Helena. In 35.0 miles, take exit 164 onto MT-69 toward Boulder. In 0.3 miles, turn right onto North Main Street. In 7.1 miles, turn left onto White Bridge Lane. In 3.1 miles, take a slight left turn onto Elkhorn Road. In 8.5 miles, turn left onto Shober Street. You have arrived at your destination.

Pekin Noodle Parlor (historical)
117 South Main Street, Butte, Montana 59701
(406)782-2217
Sunday–Thursday 11:00 a.m.–9:00 p.m.; Friday–Saturday 11:00 a.m.–10:00 p.m.
Free to look

From Bozeman, head west on I-90. In 82.0 miles, take exit 126 onto Montana Street. In 0.2 miles, turn right onto South Montana Street. In 1.2 miles, turn right onto West Mercury Street. In 0.2 miles, turn left onto South Main Street. In 150 feet, your destination will be on your left.

Granite Ghost Town (historical)
347 Granite Road, Phillipsburg, Montana 59858
(406)287-3541
Daily
Free
From Missoula, head east on I-90. In 49.0 miles, take exit 153 onto MT-1 toward Drummond. In 0.2 miles, turn right onto MT-1 toward Phillipsburg. In 26.0 miles, turn left onto West Broadway Street. In 0.8 miles, turn right onto S Sansome Street. In 0.4 miles, turn left onto Granite Road. In 0.7 miles, turn right onto Granite Road. In 2.6 miles, take a slight left turn onto County Road 169. In 0.2 miles, turn right onto County Road 169. In 500 feet, your destination will be on your right.

Garnet Ghost Town (historical; four-wheel drive recommended)

Drummond, Montana 598932

(406)329-3914

9:30 a.m.–4:30 p.m.

Free

From Missoula, head east on I-90. In 33.0 miles, take exit 138 toward Bearmouth Area. In 0.2 miles, turn left toward Bearmouth. In 0.2 miles, turn right onto Drummond Frontage Road. In 5.8 miles, turn left onto Bear Gulch Road. In 1.9 miles, keep right onto Bear Gulch Road. In 7.5 miles, keep left onto Midnight Lode Road. In 700 feet, your destination will be on your right.

Washoe Theater (historical)

305 Main Street, Anaconda, Montana

(406)563-6161

6:40 a.m.–9:30 p.m.

$5

From Butte, take I-90 West toward Missoula. In 11.0 miles, take exit 208 onto MT-1 toward Anaconda. In 8.8 miles, turn left onto Main Street. In 900 feet, your destination will be on your left.

Glendive Dinosaur and Fossil Museum (historical)

139 State Street, Glendive, Montana 59330

(406) 377-3228

Tuesday–Saturday 10:00 a.m.–5:00 p.m.

$3

From Billings, head east on I-94 toward Bismarck. In 214.0 miles, take exit 215 toward Glendive. In 0.3 miles, turn left onto North Merrill Avenue. In 900 feet, turn right onto State Street. In 450 feet, turn left. You have arrived at your destination.

Custer's Last Stand: Little Bighorn (historical)

756 Battlefield Tour Road, Crow Agency, Montana 59022

(406)638-3217

8:00 a.m.–4:30 p.m.

$25

From Billings, head east on I-90 toward Sheridan. In 54.0 miles, take exit 510 onto US-212 East toward Little Bighorn. In 0.4 miles, turn left onto US-212 toward Little Bighorn. In 0.7 miles, turn right onto Battlefield Tour Road. In 0.6 miles, you will arrive at your destination.

Old Trail Museum (historical)

823 Main Avenue N, Choteau, Montana 59422

(406)466-5332

9:00 a.m.–5:00 p.m.

$2

From Butte, head north on I-15. In 2.7 miles, take exit 129 to merge onto I-15 North toward Helena. In 45.0 miles, keep right on I-15 North. In 53.0 miles, take exit 228 onto US-287 North toward Choteau. In 39.0 miles, turn right onto Main Street. In 26.0 miles, take a slight left turn onto Seventh Avenue SW. In 0.7 miles, turn right onto Eighth Street NW. In 80 feet, turn left onto Main Avenue North. In 100 feet, turn right. You have arrived at your destination.

The World Museum of Mining (historical)

155 Mining Museum Road, Butte, Montana 59701

(406)723-7211

Tuesday–Saturday 10:00 a.m.–4:30 p.m.

$9 (museum); $21 (underground mine tour)

From Missoula, head east on I-90. In 116.0 miles, take exit 124 to merge onto I-115 East toward City Center. In 0.8 miles, take exit 1 onto South Excelsior Avenue. In 900 feet, turn left onto South Excelsior Avenue toward Walkerville. In 0.9 miles, turn left onto West Park Street. In 0.7 miles, turn left onto Mining Museum Road. In 0.2 miles, your destination will be on your right.

Roosevelt Arch Monument (historical)

Park Street, Gardiner, Montana 59030

(307)344-7381

24-7

Free

From Bozeman, head east on I-90. In 23.0 miles, take exit 333 onto US-89 South toward Yellowstone National Park. In 0.3 miles, turn left onto Park Street South toward Gardiner. In 53.0 miles, turn right onto Main Street. In 800 feet, your destination will be on your left.

Moss Mansion Museum (historical)

914 Division Street, Billings, Montana 59101

(406)256-5100

Saturday–Wednesday 12:00 p.m.–3:00 p.m.

$15

From Bozeman, head east on I-90. In 136.0 miles, take exit 446 to merge onto Laurel Road toward West Billings. In 0.3 miles, keep left on Laurel Road toward City Center. In 3.0 miles, take a slight left turn onto Division Street. In 0.2 miles, your destination will be on your left.

Havre Beneath the Streets Tour (historical)
120 3rd Avenue, Harve, Montana 59501
(406)265-8888
Monday–Sunday 10:30 a.m.–2:30 p.m.
Free
From Helena, head north on I-15 toward Great Falls. In 87.0 miles, take exit 280 onto US-87 North. In 0.3 miles, turn right onto Central Avenue West. In 1.2 miles, turn left onto Third Street NW. In 2.0 miles, turn left onto Old Havre Highway. In 0.9 miles, turn left onto US-87 North. In 107.0 miles, turn right onto US Highway 2 West. In 3.1 miles, turn right onto Third Avenue. In 200 feet, your destination will be on your right.

Thompson-Hickman Museum (historical)
220 Wallace Street, Virginia City, Montana 59755
(406)843-5238
10:00 a.m.–5:00 p.m.
Free
From Butte, head east on I-90 toward Billings. In 2.7 miles, continue onto I-90 East. In 15.0 miles, take exit 241 toward Pipestone. In 900 feet, turn right onto Pipestone Road. In 0.8 miles, turn right onto Hot Springs Road. In 3.0 miles, turn right onto SH-2 West. In 1.2 miles, take a slight left turn onto MT-41. In 8.4 miles, turn right onto Mt Highway 41 North. In 14.0 miles, continue onto Main Street. In 29.0 miles, your destination will be on your right.

Deer Lodge Old Prison Museum (historical)
1106 Main Street, Deer Lodge, Montana
(406)846-3111
Monday–Saturday 8:00 a.m.–6:00 p.m.; Sunday 9:00 a.m.–6:00 p.m. (closed during winter)
$15
From Butte, head west on I-90 toward Missoula. In 31.0 miles, take exit 187 onto I-90 BL toward Deer Lodge. In 1.6 miles, your destination will be on your left.

Conrad Mansion Museum (historical)
330 Woodland Avenue, Kalispell, Montana 59901
(406)755-2166
Tuesday–Friday 10:00 a.m.–4:00 p.m.
$17
From Missoula, head west on I-90. In 8.2 miles, take exit 96 onto US-93 North toward Kalispell. In 0.2 miles, keep right onto US-93 North. In 109.0 miles, turn right onto Willow Glen Drive. In 1.5 miles, turn left onto Woodland Avenue. In 1.1 miles, your destination will be on your left.

Pompeys Pillar (archaeological)

3039 US Highway 312, Pompeys Pillar, Montana 59064

(406)896-5013

9:00 a.m.–6:00 p.m.

$7

From Billings, head east on I-94 toward Bismarck. In 23.0 miles, take exit 23 toward Pompeys Pillar. In 0.2 miles, turn left onto South 31st Street toward Pompeys Pillar. In 0.7 miles, turn right. In 0.5 miles, you will arrive at your destination.

Pictograph Cave (archaeological)

3401 Coburn Road, Billings, Montana 59101

(406)252-7342

Wednesday–Sunday 9:00 a.m.–5:00 p.m.

$8

From Bozeman, head east on I-90. In 143.0 miles, take exit 452 onto US-87 North toward Lockwood. In 0.2 miles, turn right onto US Highway 87 East. In 200 feet, turn right onto Coburn Road. In 5.0 miles, your destination will be on your left.

Bear Gulch Pictographs (archaeological; four-wheel drive recommended)

2749 Fairview Road, Forest Grove, Montana 59411

(406)428-2185

Daily

$15

From Billings, head north on Main Street. In 3.3 miles, take a slight left turn onto Roundup Road. In 44.0 miles, turn left onto Main Street. In 0.7 miles, keep left onto US-87. In 44.0 miles, turn left onto US-87. In 17.0 miles, turn left onto North Piper Road. In 5.0 miles, turn left onto Forest Grove Road. In 7.3 miles, turn right onto Fairview Road. In 2.6 miles, prepare to park your vehicle. Your destination will be on your left.

Wyoming

Buford Wyoming Population 1 (obscure)
4095 SR-7, Buford, Wyoming
Open 24 hours
Free
From Cheyenne, head west on I-80. In 24.0 miles, take exit 335 toward Buford. In 900 feet, turn left onto Buford Road. In 500 feet, turn right onto Buford Road. In 0.5 miles, turn left onto Buford Road. In 500 feet, turn left. In 0.3 miles, you will arrive at your destination.

Smith Mansion (obscure)
2902 North Fork Highway, Cody, Wyoming 82414
(406)647-6048
Sunday 1:00 p.m.–4:00 p.m.; Monday–Friday 9:00 a.m.–5:00 p.m.; Saturday closed

Free
From Cody, head west on Yellowstone Avenue. In 23.0 miles, your destination will be on your left.

Tree in the Rock (obscure)
Interstate 80, Mile Marker 333, Buford, Wyoming 82052
24-7
Free
From Cheyenne, head west on I-80. In 30.0 miles, take exit 329 onto Vedauwoo Road. In 0.2 miles, turn left onto Vedauwoo Glen Road toward Blair Road. In 500 feet, turn left onto Cheyenne. In 3.4 miles, your destination will be on your left.

T.A. Moulton Barn (obscure)
Grand Teton National Park Mormon Row, Moose, Wyoming 83012
Open 24 hours
Free
From Jackson, take I-89 north. In 6.7 miles, turn right onto Antelope Flats Road. In 1.7 miles, turn right onto Mormon Row Road. In 0.3 miles, your destination is on your right.

Chugwater Soda Fountain (obscure)
314 1st Street, Chugwater, Wyoming 82210
(307)422-3222
8:00 a.m.–8:00 p.m.
Free
From Cheyenne, head north on I-25. In 43.0 miles, take exit 54 toward I-25 BL. In 0.3 miles, turn right onto WY-211 toward I-25 BL. In 0.3 miles, turn left onto First Street. In 0.2 miles, your destination will be on your left.

Chapel of Transfiguration (obscure)
Chapel of Transfiguration Road, Jackson, Wyoming 83001
(307)733-2603
Sunrise to sunset
Free
From Jackson, head north on US-89. In 5.5 miles, turn left onto Teton Park Road. In 1.0 mile, keep right onto Teton Park Road. In 0.3 miles, turn right onto Chapel of Transfiguration Road. In 0.4 miles, your destination will be on your left.

Castle Geyser (nature)
Upper Geyser Basin Trail, Alta, Wyoming 83414
Open 24 hours
Park fee $35
From Moran, take I-89 north. In 48.0 miles, turn right onto US-20. In 21.0 miles, continue onto Grand Loop Road. In 15.0 miles, turn left onto Norris Canyon Road. In 12.0 miles, turn left onto Grand Loop Road. In 29.0 miles, prepare to park your vehicle. Take a left onto Punch Bowl-Black Sand Basin Trail. In 0.8 miles, turn right onto UGB-Biscuit Basin Trail. In 0.55 miles, take a left onto Upper Geyser Basin Trail. In 190 feet, your destination will be on your right.

Intermittent Springs (nature)
5 East 2nd Avenue, Afton, Wyoming 83110
Daily
Free
From Jackson, take US-89 south. In 23.0 miles, turn left onto US-89. In 33.0 miles, turn left onto East 2nd Street. In 25 feet, your destination will be on your left.

Cheyenne Botanic Gardens (nature)
710 S Lions Park Drive, Cheyenne, Wyoming 82001
(307)637-6458
Tuesday–Saturday 10:00 a.m.–3:00 p.m.
Free
From Casper, head south on I-25 toward Cheyenne. In 175.0 miles, take exit 12 onto US-85 South. In 0.3 miles, turn left onto Central Avenue toward Business I-25. In 0.6 miles, turn right onto Kennedy Road. In 0.2 miles, turn left onto Carey Avenue. In 0.5 miles, turn left onto South Lions Park Drive. In 250 feet, turn left into the parking lot. In 300 feet, your destination will be on your right.

Devils Tower (nature)
149 State Highway 110, Devils Tower, Wyoming 827714
(307)467-5283
Open 24 hours
$25
From Casper, head north on I-25 toward Buffalo. In 22.0 miles, take exit 210 onto WY-259. In 0.3 miles, turn right onto WY-259 toward Midwest. In 18.0 miles, turn right onto WY-387. In 32.0 miles, turn left onto WY-50. In 51.0 miles, turn right to merge onto I-90 East toward Moorcroft. In 30.0 miles, take exit 154. In 700 feet, turn right toward Moorcroft. In 0.2 miles, turn right onto East Converse Street. In 0.2 miles, turn right onto North Yellowstone Avenue. In 4.9 miles, keep left onto US-14. In 21.0 miles, turn left onto WY-24. In 6.0 miles, turn left onto WY-110. In 3.5 miles, prepare to park your vehicle. Take a right onto Tower. In 0.5 miles, you will arrive at your destination.

Mystic Falls (nature)
Biscuit Basin Trail, Alta, Wyoming 83414
Open 24 hours
Park Fee $35

From Moran, take I-89 north. In 48.0 miles, turn right onto US-20. In 21.0 miles, continue onto Grand Loop Road. In 15.0 miles, turn left onto Norris Canyon Road. In 12.0 miles, turn left onto Grand Loop Road. In 27.0 miles, turn right. In 900 feet, your destination will be on your right.

Old Faithful (nature)

Upper Geyser Basin, Alta Wyoming 83414

(307)344-7381

Open 24 hours

Park Fee $35

From Moran, head north US-89. In 48.0 miles, turn right onto US-20. In 21.0 miles, turn left onto Grand Loop Road. In 15.0 miles, turn left onto Norris Canyon Road. In 12.0 miles, turn left onto Grand Loop Road. In 29.0 miles, prepare to park your vehicle near Punch Bowl-Black Sand Basin Trail. Take a left onto Punch Bowl-Black Sand Basin Trail. In 0.8 miles, turn right onto UGB-Biscuit Basin Trail. In 1.1 miles, turn right. In 180 feet, turn right. In 360 feet, you will arrive at your destination.

Lone Star Geyser (nature)

Lone Star Trail, Alta, Wyoming 83414

Open 24 hours

Park Fee $35

From Moran, take US-89 north. In 48.0 miles, continue onto Grand Loop Road. In 15.0 miles, turn left. In 350 feet, your destination will be on your right.

Boars Tusk Rock Formation (nature; hiking required)

Chilton Road, Farson, Wyoming 82932

24-7

Free

From Rock Springs, head north on Elk Street. In 4.4 miles, keep left onto US-191. In 5.9 miles, turn right onto County Road 17. In 5.0 miles, keep left onto County Road 17. In 9.9 miles, take a slight left turn. In 4.7 miles, prepare to park your vehicle. Head right. In 2.5 miles, you will arrive near your destination.

Hell's Half Acre (nature)

Hell's Half Acre Road, Powder River, Wyoming 82604

Daily

Free

From Casper, take Yellowstone Highway west. In 39.0 miles, turn left onto Hell's Half Acre Road. In 300 feet, you will arrive at your destination.

Sapphire Pool (nature; hiking required)

Biscuit Basin Trail, Alta, Wyoming 83414

Open 24 hours

Park fee $35

From Moran, take I-89 north. In 48.0 miles, turn right onto US-20. In 21.0 miles, continue onto Grand Loop Road. In 15.0 miles, turn left onto Norris Canyon Road. In 12.0 miles, turn left onto Grand Loop Road. In 27.0 miles, turn right. In 900 feet, prepare to park your vehicle. Continue onto Biscuit Basin Trail. In 780 feet, your destination will be on your right.

Morning Glory Pool (nature)
Yellowstone National Park, UGB-Biscuit Trail, Alta, Wyoming 83414
Open 24 hours
Park Fee $35
From Jackson, take US-89 north. In 48.0 miles, turn right onto US-20. In 21.0 miles, continue onto Grand Loop Road. In 15.0 miles, turn left onto Norris Canyon Road. In 12.0 miles, turn left onto Grand Loop Road. In 27.0 miles, prepare to park your car near UGB-Biscuit Trail. Follow UGB-Biscuit trail for 0.75 miles, then you will arrive at your destination.

Fairy Falls (nature; hiking required)
Fairy Falls Trail, Alta, Wyoming 84314
Open 24 hours
Park fee $35
From Moran, take I-89 north. In 48.0 miles, turn right onto US-20. In 21.0 miles, continue onto Grand Loop Road. In 15.0 miles, turn left onto Norris Canyon Road. In 12.0 miles, turn left onto Grand Loop Road. In 25.0 miles, turn right. In 350 feet, turn right. In 150 feet, prepare to park your vehicle near Fairy Falls Trail. Take a slight right to turn onto Fairy Falls Trail. In 200 feet, you will arrive at your destination.

Firehole Canyon (nature; hiking required)
Firehole Canyon, Alta, Wyoming 83013
Open 24 hours
Park fee $35
From Moran, take I-89 north. In 48.0 miles, turn right onto US-20. In 21.0 miles, continue onto Grand Loop Road. In 15.0 miles, turn left onto Norris Canyon Road. In 12.0 miles, turn left onto Grand Loop Road. In 12.0 miles, turn left onto Grand Loop Road. In 14.0 miles, turn right onto Firehole Canyon Road. In 0.3 miles, prepare to park your vehicle.

The Grand Tetons (nature)
403 S Jenny Lake Drive, Jackson, Wyoming 83001
(307)739-3399
24-7
$15
From Jackson, head north on US Highway 89. In 5.5 miles, turn left onto Teton Park Road. In 1.0 mile, keep right. In 6.9 miles, turn left. In 0.3 miles, your destination will be on your right.

Gibbon Falls (nature)
Grand Loop Road, Alta, Wyoming 83013
(307)344-7381
Open 24 hours
Park fee $35
From Moran, take I-89 north. In 48.0 miles, turn right onto US-20. In 21.0 miles, continue onto Grand Loop Road. In 15.0 miles, turn left onto Norris Canyon Road. In 12.0 miles, turn left onto Grand Loop Road. In 12.0 miles, turn left onto Grand Loop Road. In 8.5 miles, your destination will be on your left.

Grand Prismatic Spring (nature; hiking required)
Yellowstone National Park, Alta, Wyoming 83013
(307)344-7381
Sunday 8:00 a.m.–8:00 p.m.; Saturday 8:00 a.m.–8:00 p.m.
Park fee $35
From Jackson, take US-89 north. In 48.0 miles, turn right onto US-20. In 21.0 miles, continue onto Grand Loop Road. In 15.0 miles, turn left onto Norris Canyon Road. In 12.0 miles, turn left onto Grand Loop Road. In 24.0 miles, prepare to park your vehicle. Continue onto Midway Geyser Basin Trail. In 880 feet, take a left onto Midway Geyser Basin Trail. In 720 feet, your destination will be on your left.

Buffalo Bill Center of the West (historical)
720 Sheridan Avenue, Cody, Wyoming 82414
(307)587-4771
8:00 a.m.–6:00 p.m.
$19.50
From Sheridan, head west on US-14 toward Billings. In 14.0 miles, take exit 9 onto US-14 West toward Ranchester. In 0.4 miles, turn left onto US-14. In 79.0 miles, turn right onto North Sixth Street. In 54.0 miles, turn right. You have arrived at your destination.

Wyoming Frontier Prison Museum (historical)
500 W Walnut Street, Rawlins, Wyoming 82301
(307)324-4422
Monday–Thursday 9:00 a.m.–1:00 a.m.; Friday–Sunday 10:30 a.m.–10:30 p.m.
$10
From Cheyenne, head west on I-80. In 143.0 miles, take exit 215 onto US-287 North toward I-80 BL. In 2.4 miles, turn right onto 3rd Street. In 0.3 miles, turn left onto West Walnut Street. In 700 feet, your destination will be on your left.

Old Trail Town (historical)
1831 Demaris Street, Cody, Wyoming 82414
(307)587-5302
8:00 a.m.–6:00 p.m.
$10
From Sheridan, head west on US-14 toward Billings. In 14.0 miles, take exit 9 onto US-14 West toward Ranchester. In 0.4 miles, turn left onto US-14. In 79.0 miles, turn right onto North 6th Street. In 56.0 miles, turn right onto Demaris Street. In 500 feet, turn left. Your destination will be on your right.

Cheyenne Depot Museum (historical)
121 W 15th Street, Unit 300, Cheyenne, Wyoming 82001
(307)632-3905
Monday–Friday 9:00 a.m.–5:00 p.m.; Saturday 9:00 a.m.–3:00 p.m.; Sunday 11:00 a.m.–3:00 p.m.
$8
From Casper, head south on I-25. In 177.0 miles, take exit 10D onto Missile Drive. In 0.3 miles, turn right onto Missile Drive. In 1.0 mile, turn left onto West Lincolnway. In 0.7 miles, turn right onto Capitol Avenue. In 350 feet, turn left onto West 15th Street. Your destination will be on your right.

Ames Brothers Pyramid (historical)

211-205 Monument Road, Buford, Wyoming

(307)-777-6323

Daily

Free

From Cheyenne, head west on I-80. In 30.0 miles, take exit 329 onto Vedauwoo Road. In 0.2 miles, turn left onto Vedauwoo Glen Road. In 700 feet, turn left onto Monument Road. In 1.9 miles, turn right. In 500 feet, you will arrive at your destination.

National Historic Trails Interpretive Center (historical)

1501 N Poplar Street, Casper, Wyoming 82601

(307)261-7700

Tuesday–Saturday 9:00 a.m.–4:30 p.m.

Free

From Cheyenne, head north on I-25 toward Casper. In 178.0 miles, take exit 189 onto US-20 toward Events Center. In 0.3 miles, keep right onto Events Drive. In 0.3 miles, turn right onto North Poplar Street. In 350 feet, turn left. In 400 feet, turn right into the parking lot. You have arrived at your destination.

Wyoming Territorial Prison Historic Site (historical)
975 Snowy Range Road, Laramie, Wyoming 82072
(307)745-6161
Wednesday–Saturday 10:00 a.m.–3:00 p.m.
$7.50
From Cheyenne, head west on I-80. In 47.0 miles, take exit 311 onto WY-230. In 0.3 miles, turn right onto Snowy Range Road. In 0.3 miles, turn left. You have arrived at your destination.

Fort Bridger Historic Site (historical)
37000 I-80 BL, Fort Bridger, Wyoming 82933
(307)782-3842
Wednesday–Sunday 9:00 a.m.–5:00 p.m.
$7
From Rock Springs, head west on I-80 toward Green River. In 62.0 miles, take exit onto WY-412. In 0.3 miles, turn left onto WY-412 toward Mountain View. In 2.9 miles, turn right onto I-80 BL. In 2.7 miles, your destination will be on your right.

Hole in the Wall Hideout (historical; four-wheel drive; high clearance ONLY; remote mountain pass; hiking required)
Kaycee, Wyoming 82639
Daily
Free
From Casper, head north on I-25 toward Buffalo. In 66.0 miles, take exit 254 toward Kaycee. In 0.2 miles, turn left onto Mayoworth Road toward Mayoworth. In 1.0 mile, turn left onto Barnum Road. In 16.0 miles, stay left onto Barnum Mountain Road. In 0.4 miles, stay left onto Bar-C Road. In 4.6 miles, prepare to park your vehicle near Bar-C Road. In 4.9 miles, you will arrive at your destination.

Independence Rock (historical)
WY-220, Alcova, Wyoming 82620
(307)577-5150
Open 24 hours
Free
From Casper, take WY-220 north. In 45.0 miles, turn left. Prepare to park your vehicle. Walk over the bridge. In 760 feet, take a left. In 50 feet, you will arrive at your destination.

Big Horn Medicine Wheel (archaeological; four-wheel drive recommended; hiking required)
Big Horn National Forest, Lovell, Wyoming 82431
June–October; open 24 hours (closed during winter)
Free
From Sheridan, head west on US-14 toward Billings. In 14.0 miles, take exit 9 onto US-14 West. In 0.4 miles, turn left onto US-14 toward Lovell. In 79.0 miles, turn right onto North Sixth Street. In 5.0 miles, turn right onto US-310. In 27.0 miles, turn right onto US Highway 14A East. In 22.0 miles, turn left onto Old US Highway 14A. In 2.1 miles, turn right. In 200 feet, prepare to park your vehicle. Continue right onto trail head. In 1.30 miles, your destination will be on your left.

Woods Landing Bar and Cafe (historical)
9 WY-10, Jelm, Wyoming 82063
(307)745-5770
Monday–Saturday 11:00 a.m.–8:00 p.m.; Sunday 8:00 a.m.–8:00 p.m.
Free to look
From Cheyenne, take I-80 west. In 47.0 miles, take exit 311 onto Snowy Range Road. In 0.3 miles, turn left onto Snowy Range Road toward Woods Landing. In 26.0 miles, turn left onto WY-10. In 700 feet, your destination will be on your right.

Register Cliff (historical; follow signs from parking area)
257 South Guernsey Road, Hartville, Wyoming 82214
Open daily
Free
From Cheyenne, take I-25 North for 81.0 miles. In 53.0 miles, take exit 92 onto US-26 East toward Guernsey. In 15.0 miles, turn right onto South Wyoming Avenue. In 2.6 miles, turn left. In 0.5 miles, turn right. In 600 feet, prepare to park your vehicle.

Aladdin Coal Tipple (historical)
Aladdin, Wyoming 82710
Open 24 hours
Free
From Gillette take I-90 east toward Moorcroft. In 72.0 miles, take exit 199 for WY-111 toward Aladdin. In 0.4 miles, turn left onto WY-111 North. In 8.7 miles, turn right onto WY-24 East. In 1.5 miles, your destination will be on your left.

Guernsey Ruts (archaeological)
Hartville, Wyoming 82215
(307)836-2334
24-7
Free
From Cheyenne, head north on I-25. In 81.0 miles, take exit 92 onto US-26 East toward Guernsey. In 15.0 miles, turn right. In 0.8 miles, turn right. In 0.2 miles, prepare to park your vehicle

Castle Garden Petroglyph Site (archaeological; hiking required)
Lander, Wyoming 82520
(307)382-8400
24-7
Free
From Casper, head west on Yellowstone Highway. In 72.0 miles, turn left onto Castle Gardens Road. In 15.0 miles, prepare to park your vehicle. Head left. In 5.7 miles, your destination will be on your right.

Hell Gap (archaeological)
635-673 Whalen Canyon Road, Fort Laramie, Wyoming 82212
Daily
Free
From Casper, head south on I-25. In 95.0 miles, take exit 92 onto US-26 East toward Guernsey. In 17.0 miles, turn left onto WY-270. In 2.5 miles, turn right onto Whalen Canyon Road. In 8.2 miles, you will arrive at your destination.

North Dakota

The Enchanted Highway (obscure)
102nd Avenue SW, Mott, North Dakota 58650
Open 24 hours
Free
From Gladstone, follow ND-22 South for 31.0 miles, ending in Regent.

Plains Art Museum (obscure)
704 First Avenue N, Fargo, North Dakota 58102
(705)551-6100
Monday–Wednesday 11:00 a.m.–5:00 p.m.; Thursday 11:00 a.m.–9:00 p.m.
Friday–Saturday 10:00 a.m.–5:00 p.m.
Free

From Bismarck, head east on I-94 toward Fargo. In 97.0 miles, continue onto Truck US-281 South. In 95.0 miles, take exit 351 onto Bus US-81 toward downtown. In 0.3 miles, turn left onto University Drive South. In 1.0 mile, turn right onto 13th Avenue South. In 700 feet, turn left onto 10th Street South. In 1.1 miles, turn right onto 1st Avenue North. In 500 feet, your destination will be on your right.

Keelboat Park (obscure)

1605 River Road, Bismarck, North Dakota 58503
Monday–Friday 8:00 a.m.–10:00 p.m.
Free
From Fargo, head west on I-94. In 194.0 miles, take exit 157 toward Divide Avenue. In 0.3 miles, turn right onto Tyler Parkway. In 700 feet, turn left onto Burnt Boat Drive. In 0.8 miles, turn left onto River Road. In 0.6 miles, your destination will be on your right.

Gateway to Science Museum (obscure)

1810 Schafer Street Unit 1, Bismarck, North Dakota 58501
(701)258-1975
Monday–Thursday 12:00 p.m.–7:00 p.m.; Friday–Saturday 10:00 a.m.–5:00 p.m.
$9
From Fargo, head west on I-94. In 194.0 miles, take exit 157 toward Divide Avenue. In 0.3 miles, turn left onto Tyler Parkway. In 0.2 miles, turn right onto Schafer Street. In 700 feet, your destination will be on your right.

National Buffalo Museum/World's Largest Buffalo (obscure)

500 17th Street SE, Jamestown, North Dakota 58401
(800)222-4766
10:00 a.m.–6:00 p.m.
Free
From Fargo, take I-94 West toward Jamestown. In 93.0 miles, take exit 258 onto US-281 toward Jamestown. In 0.3 miles, turn right onto US-281 North. In 0.3 miles, turn right onto 17th Street SW. In 0.8 miles, turn right. In 150 feet, your destination will be on your left.

Fargo Wood Chipper (obscure)
2001 44th Street South, Fargo, North Dakota 58103
(701)282-3653
Monday–Friday 9:00 a.m.–4:00 p.m.; Saturday 10:00 a.m.–4:00 p.m.; Sunday closed
Free
From Bismarck, head east on I-94 toward Fargo. In 97.0 miles, continue onto Truck US-281 South. In 92 miles, take exit 348 onto 45th Street. In 0.3 miles, turn left onto 45th Street South. In 0.3 miles, turn right onto 19th Avenue South. In 600 feet, turn right onto 44th Street South. In 400 feet, turn right into the parking lot. You have arrived at your destination.

Paul Broste Rock Museum (obscure)
Sixth Avenue NE, Parshall, North Dakota
(701)862-3264
Wednesday–Saturday 12:00 p.m.–4:00 p.m.
$5
From Bismarck, head west on I-94 toward Billings. In 7.9 miles, take exit 147 onto ND-25 toward Center Stanton. In 0.2 miles, turn right onto ND-25. In 19.0 miles, turn right onto 28th Avenue SW. In 11.0 miles, turn right onto SH-200 Alt. In 4.4 miles, turn left onto US-83 North. In 51.0 miles, turn left onto 247th Avenue SE. In 39.0 miles, turn left onto 72nd Avenue NW. In 1.0 mile, turn right onto 38th Street NW. In 0.2 miles, turn left onto Main Street North. In 600 feet, turn left onto Sixth Avenue NE. In 200 feet, you will arrive at your destination.

Salem Sue World's Largest Holstein Cow (obscure)
8th Avenue North, New Salem, North Dakota 58563
(701)843-7828
Open 24 hours
Free
From Bismarck, take I-94 west toward Billings. In 27.0 miles, take exit 127 onto ND-31 North toward New Salem. In 0.2 miles, turn left onto ND-31. In 0.5 miles, turn right. In 450 feet, turn right. In 800 feet, prepare to park your vehicle. Your destination will be on your right.

Tommy the Turtle (obscure)
1001 10th Street E, Bottineau, North Dakota 58318
Daily
Free
From Bismarck, head west on I-94 toward Billings. In 7.9 miles, take exit 147 onto ND-25 toward Center Station. In 0.2 miles, turn right onto ND-25. In 19.0 miles, turn right onto 28th Avenue

SW. In 11.0 miles, turn right onto SH-200 Alt. In 4.4 miles, turn left onto US-83 North. In 106.0 miles, turn right onto 93rd Street NW. In 6.6 miles, continue onto US-83. In 37.0 miles, turn left onto Jay Street South. In 600 feet, your destination will be on your right.

Scandinavian Heritage Association/Gol Stave Church Museum (obscure)

1020 S Broadway, Minot, North Dakota 58701
(701) 852-9161
Monday–Friday 9:00 a.m.–4:00 p.m.
Donations
From Bismarck, head west on I-94 toward Billings. In 7.9 miles, take exit 147 onto ND-25 toward Center Stanton. In 0.2 miles, turn right onto ND25. In 19.0 miles, turn right onto 28th Avenue SW. In 11.0 miles, turn right onto SH-200 Alt. In 4.4 miles, turn left onto US-83 North. In 68.0 miles, turn left onto 11th Avenue SW. In 100 feet, your destination will be on your right.

Medicine Wheel Park (obscure)

Second Avenue SE, Valley City, North Dakota 58072
Sunrise to sunset
Free
From Fargo, head west on I-94. In 59.0 miles, take exit 292 toward Valley City. In 0.2 miles, turn right onto 8th Avenue SW. In 400 feet, turn right onto Winter Show Road SW. In 0.5 miles, turn left onto 2nd Avenue SE. In 400 feet, your destination will be on your right.

Children's Museum at Yunker Farm (obscure)

1201 28th Avenue N, Fargo, North Dakota 58102
(701)232-6102
10:00 a.m.–5:00 p.m.
$5
From Bismarck, head east on I-94 toward Fargo. In 97.0 miles, continue onto Truck US-281 South. In 93.0 miles, take exit 349B onto US-81 North toward Grand Forks. In 4.0 miles, take exit 67 onto US-81. In 0.3 miles, keep right onto Bus US-81 toward Hector International Airport. In 1.9 miles, turn left onto University Drive North. In 0.5 miles, turn right onto 28th Avenue North. In 450 feet, turn left. Your destination will be on your left.

W'eel Turtle Sculpture (obscure)

Main Street, Dunseith, North Dakota 58329
Daily

Free

From Bismarck, head south on US-83 toward Fargo. In 23.0 miles, take exit 182 onto US-83 South toward Sterling. In 0.3 miles, turn left onto 314th Street. In 900 feet, continue onto 314th Street. In 73.0 miles, continue onto County Road 11. In 10.0 miles, turn right onto 42nd Street NE. In 14.0 miles, turn left onto ND-3. In 25.0 miles, turn left onto 1st Street NW. In 31.0 miles, turn left onto ND-5. In 0.4 miles, turn right onto Main Street. In 450 feet, turn left onto 1st Street NW. In 400 feet, take a slight right turn. Your destination will be on your right.

Geographical Center of North America (obscure)
120 Highway 2 SW, Rugby, North Dakota 58368
(701)776-5846
Daily
Free to look
From Bismarck, take US-83 south toward Fargo. In 23.0 miles, take exit 182 onto US-83 South toward Sterling. In 0.3 miles, turn left onto 314th Street. In 900 feet, continue onto 314th Street. In 73.0 miles, continue onto County Road 11. In 10.0 miles, turn right onto 42nd Street NE. In 14.0 miles, turn left onto ND-3. In 24.0 miles, turn right onto 29th Avenue NE. In 100 feet, your destination will be on your left.

International Peace Garden (nature)
US-281 S, Dunseith, North Dakota 58329
(701)263-4390
10:00 a.m.–4:00 p.m.
$20
From Bismarck, head south on US-83 toward Fargo. In 23.0 miles, take exit 182 onto US-83 South toward Sterling. In 0.3 miles, turn left onto 314th Street. In 900 feet, continue onto 314th Street. In 73.0 miles, continue onto County Road 11. In 10.0 miles, turn right onto 42nd Street NE. In 14.0 miles, turn left onto ND-3. In 25.0 miles, turn left onto 1st Street NW. In 31.0 miles, turn left onto ND-5. In 0.4 miles, turn right onto Main Street. In 14.0 miles, turn left. In 150 feet, your destination will be on your left.

Lake Sakakawea State Park (nature)
720 Park Avenue, Hazen, North Dakota 58545
(701)487-3315
Sunrise to sunset
$7

From Bismarck, head west on I-94 toward Billings. In 7.9 miles, take exit 147 onto ND-25 toward Center Stanton. In 0.2 miles, turn right onto ND-25. In 19.0 miles, turn right onto 28th Avenue SW. In 11.0 miles, turn right onto SH-200 Alt. In 4.4 miles, turn left onto US-83 North. In 16.0 miles, turn left onto Sixth Street NW. In 14.0 miles, turn right onto Park Avenue. In 1.3 miles, turn left. In 300 feet, turn left. In 300 feet, your destination will be on your left.

Lake Metigoshe State Park (nature)
2 Lake Metigoshe Park Road, Bottineau, North Dakota 58318
(701)263-4651
Sunrise to sunset
$7
From Bismarck, head west on I-94. In 1.8 miles, keep right on I-94 West toward Billings. In 7.9 miles, take exit 147 onto ND-25 toward Center Stanton. In 0.2 miles, turn right onto ND-25. In 19.0 miles, turn right onto 28th Avenue SW. In 11.0 miles, turn right onto SH-200 Alt. In 4.4 miles, turn left onto US-83 North. In 106.0 miles, turn right onto 93rd Street NW. In 6.6 miles, continue onto US-83. In 35.0 miles, turn left onto 11th Avenue NE. In 1.0 mile, turn right onto 98th Street NE. In 1.0 mile, turn left onto County Road 49. In 8.0 miles, turn right onto ND-43. In 4.5 miles, turn left onto Lake Loop Road East. In 2.2 miles, turn right onto East Shore Park Road. In 200 feet, your destination will be on your right.

Fort Ransom State Park (nature)
5981 119th Avenue SE, Fort Ransom, North Dakota 58033
(701)973-4331
Sunrise to sunset
$7
From Fargo, head west on I-94. In 49.0 miles, take exit onto 127th Avenue SE. In 0.3 miles, turn left onto 127th Avenue SE. In 21.0 miles, turn right onto 54th Street SE. In 1.8 miles, turn left onto 123rd Avenue SE. In 4.0 miles, turn right onto 58th Street SE. In 2.0 miles, take a slight left turn onto Valley Road. In 2.8 miles, turn right onto Walt Hjelle Parkway. Your destination will be on your right.

Theodore Roosevelt National Park (nature)

315 2nd Avenue, Medora, North Dakota 58645

(701)623-4466

24-7

$25

From Bismarck, head west on I-94 toward Billings. In 122.0 miles, take exit 32 toward Painted Canyon Visitor Center. In 0.2 miles, turn right. In 400 feet, your destination will be on your left.

Chateau De Mores State Historic Site (historical)

3426 Chateau Road, Medora, North Dakota 58645

(701)623-4355

Tuesday–Saturday 9:00 a.m.–5:00 p.m.

$10

From Bismarck, head west on I-94 toward Billings. In 128.0 miles, take exit 27 onto I-94 BL toward Medora. In 2.4 miles, turn left onto Chateau Road. In 0.2 miles, your destination will be on your left.

Fort Buford State Historic Site (historical)

15349 39th Lane NW, Williston, North Dakota 58801

(701)572-9034

10:00 a.m.–6:00 p.m.

$5

From Bismark, head west on I-94. In 112.0 miles, take exit 42 onto US-85 toward Belfield. In 0.2 miles, turn right onto US-85. In 87.0 miles, turn left onto ND-200. In 18.0 miles, at the round-about, take the first exit onto ND-58 North. In 9.7 miles, continue onto ND-1804. In 0.5 miles, turn right onto 153rd Avenue NW. In 0.9 miles, turn right onto Thirty-Ninth Lane NW. In 0.5 miles, turn right, your destination will be at your right.

Fort Union Trading Post (historical)

15550 Highway 1804, Williston, North Dakota 58801

(701)572-9083

9:00 a.m.–5:00 p.m.

Free

From Bismarck, head west on I-94. In 112.0 miles, take exit 42 onto US-85 toward Belfield. In 0.2 miles, turn right onto US-85. In 87.0 miles, turn left onto ND-200. In 18.0 miles, at the round-about, take the first exit onto ND-58 North. In 9.7 miles, continue onto ND-1804. In 1.8 miles, your destination will be on your left.

Fort Abraham Lincoln State Park (historical)

4480 Fort Lincoln Road, Mandan, North Dakota 58554

(701)667-6340

Tuesday–Saturday 10:00 a.m.–5:00 p.m.

$7

From Fargo, head west on I-94. In 196.0 miles, take exit 155 onto Main Street. In 0.7 miles, continue onto East Main Street. In 0.7 miles, turn left onto 6th Avenue SE. In 7.0 miles, turn left onto Fort Lincoln Road. In 0.6 miles, you will arrive at your destination.

Bonanzaville USA History Museum (historical)

1351 Main Avenue NW, West Fargo, North Dakota 58078

(701)282-2282

Monday–Friday 10:00 a.m.–8:00 p.m.; Saturday 10:00 a.m.–5:00 p.m.

$12

From Bismarck, head east on I-94 toward Fargo. In 97.0 miles, continue onto Truck US-281 South. In 87.0 miles, take exit 343 onto US-10. In 1.5 miles, turn right onto 15th Street NW. In 400 feet, turn right. You have arrived at your destination.

Fort Mandan (historical)
8th Street SW, Mandan, North Dakota 58577
(701)462-8535
Tuesday–Saturday 10:00 a.m.–5:00 p.m.
$8
From Bismarck, head west on I-94 toward Billings. In 7.9 miles, take exit 147 onto ND-25 toward Center Stanton. In 0.2 miles, turn right onto ND-25. In 19.0 miles, turn right onto 28th Avenue SW. In 11.0 miles, turn right onto SH-200 Alt. In 4.3 miles, turn left onto 8th Street SW. In 2.4 miles, turn left onto 8th Street SW. In 0.2 miles, your destination will be on your left.

Dakota Territory Air Museum (historical)
100 34th Avenue SE, Minot, North Dakota 58702
(701)852-8500
Monday–Saturday 10:00 a.m.–5:00 p.m.; Sunday 1:00 p.m.–5:00 p.m.
$10
From Bismarck, head west on I-94 toward Billings. In 7.9 miles, take exit 147 onto ND-25 toward Center Stanton. In 0.2 miles, turn right onto ND-25. In 19.0 miles, turn right onto 28th Avenue SW. In 11.0 miles, turn right onto SH 200 Alt. In 4.4 miles, turn left onto US-83 North. In 72.0 miles, turn right onto 34th Avenue NW. In 0.2 miles, turn right. You have arrived at your destination.

North Dakota Cowboy Hall of Fame (historical)
250 Main Street, Medora, North Dakota 58645
(701)623-2000
Tuesday–Sunday 10:00 a.m.–4:00 p.m.
$9
From Bismarck, head west on I-94 toward Billings. In 128.0 miles, take exit 27 onto I-94 BL toward Medora. In 2.0 miles, turn right onto Main Street. In 400 feet, your destination will be on your left.

Fort Totten State Historic Site (historical)
417 Calvary Circle, Fort Totten, North Dakota 58335
(701)766-4441
10:00 a.m.–5:00 p.m.
$4
From Fargo, head north on I-29 toward Grand Forks. In 76.0 miles, take exit 141 onto Gateway Drive. In 0.2 miles, turn left onto Gateway Drive toward Grand Forks AFB. In 86.0 miles, turn left onto ND-20. In 5.0 miles, continue onto ND-57. In 7.0 miles, turn left onto Indian Route 7. In 0.7

miles, continue straight. In 0.2 miles, turn left onto Calvary Circle. In 200 feet, you will arrive at your destination.

Camp Hancock State Historic Site (historical)

101 E Main Avenue, Bismarck, North Dakota 58501

(701)328-2666

Sunrise to sunset (site grounds and interpretive signs); museum (appointment only)

Free

From Fargo, head west on I-94 toward Bismarck. In 192.0 miles, take exit 159 onto US-83 North toward Bismarck. In 0.2 miles, turn left onto State Street. In 700 feet, continue onto State Street. In 1.2 miles, turn left onto North Seventh Street. In 0.8 miles, turn right onto East Main Avenue. In 0.4 miles, your destination will be on your left.

Dickinson Museum Center & Badlands Dinosaur Museum (historical)

188 Museum Drive E, Dickinson, North Dakota 58601

(701)385-4046

Monday–Saturday 9:00 a.m.–5:00 p.m.

$6

From Bismarck, head west on I-94 toward Billings. In 93.0 miles, take exit 61 onto ND-22 toward Dickinson. In 0.2 miles, turn left onto 3rd Avenue West. In 0.2 miles, turn left onto Museum Drive West. In 0.2 miles, turn left into the parking lot. You have arrived at your destination.

Lewis and Clark Interpretive Center (historical)

2576 8th Street SW, Washburn, North Dakota 58577

(701)462-8535

Tuesday–Saturday 10:00 a.m.–5:00 p.m.

$5

From Bismarck, head west on I-94 toward Billings. In 7.9 miles, take exit 147 onto ND-25 toward Center Stanton. In 0.2 miles, turn right onto ND-25. In 19.0 miles, turn right onto 28th Avenue SW. In 11.0 miles, turn right onto SH 200 Alt. In 4.3 miles, turn left onto 8th Street SW. In 0.2 miles, your destination will be on our left.

Pembina State Museum (historical)

805 ND-59, Pembina, North Dakota 58271

(701)825-6840

Tuesday–Saturday 9:00 a.m.–5:00 p.m.

$2
From Fargo, head north on I-29 toward Grand Forks. In 150.0 miles, take exit 215 onto ND-59 toward County Road 55. In 0.2 miles, turn right onto West Stutsman Street toward Pembina State Museum and Park. In 200 feet, turn left onto ND-59. In 0.2 miles, your destination will be on your left.

McKenzie County Heritage Park (historical)

950 2nd Avenue SW, Watford City, North Dakota 58854
(701)842-6434
Memorial Day–Labor Day; Wednesday–Sunday 10:00 a.m.–6:00 p.m.
Free
From Bismarck, head west on I-94 toward Billings. In 112.0 miles, take exit 42 onto US-85 toward Watford City. In 0.2 miles, turn right onto US-85. In 63.0 miles, take a slight right turn onto ND-23. In 0.6 miles, turn left onto Bus US-85. In 2.1 miles, turn left onto 2nd Avenue SW. In 0.6 miles, turn right. In 100 feet, turn left. In 200 feet, your destination will be on your left.

Killdeer Mountain Battlefield State Historic Site (historical)

Killdeer Mountain Battlefield Road, Killdeer, North Dakota 58640
(701)328-2666
Monday–Friday 8:00 a.m.–5:00 p.m.; Saturday–Sunday 10:00 a.m.–5:00 p.m.
Free
From Bismarck, head west on I-94 toward Billings. In 93.0 miles, take exit 61 onto ND-22 toward Killdeer. In 0.2 miles, keep right onto ND-22. In 32.0 miles, at the roundabout, take the third exit onto 4th Street. In 2.0 miles, at the roundabout, take the first exit onto 4th Street. In 3.0 miles, turn left onto 1st Street SW. In 4.0 miles, turn right onto 105th Avenue NW. In 1.0 mile, turn left onto Killdeer Mountain Battlefield Road. In 1.8 miles, prepare to park your vehicle.

Ronald Reagan Minuteman Missile Site and Museum (historical)

555 113-1/2 Avenue NE Highway 45, Cooperstown, North Dakota 58425
(701)797-3691
10:00 a.m.–6:00 p.m.
$10
From Fargo, head north on I-29 toward Grand Forks. In 20.0 miles, take exit 85 toward Gardner. In 0.2 miles, turn left onto 18th Street SE. In 29.0 miles, turn right onto 138th Street. In 17.0 miles, turn right onto ND-32. In 8.8 miles, turn left onto 2nd Street NE. In 14.0 miles, turn right onto 9th Street SE. In 4.1 miles, turn left. In 700 feet, you will arrive at your destination.

The First Mosque in America (historical)
5005–5099 87th Avenue NW, Ross, North Dakota 58784
Sunrise to sunset
Donation
From Bismarck, head North on US-83 toward Minot. In 106.0 miles, take a slight right turn onto US-2 West. In 60.0 miles, turn left onto 87th Avenue NW. In 0.5 miles, your destination will be on your right.

North Dakota Heritage Center & State Museum (historical)
612 E Boulevard Avenue, Bismarck, North Dakota 58505
(701)328-2666
Monday–Friday 9:00 a.m.–4:00 p.m.; Saturday–Sunday 11:00 a.m.–4:00 p.m.
Free
From Fargo, head west on I-94 toward Bismarck. In 192.0 miles, take exit 159 onto US-83 North toward Bismarck. In 0.2 miles, turn left onto State Street. In 700 feet, continue onto State Street. In 0.8 miles, turn right. In 250 feet, you will arrive at your destination.

Pioneer Trails Regional Museum (historical)
12 1st Avenue NE, Bowman, North Dakota 58623
(701)523-3600
Monday–Friday 10:00 a.m.–6:00 p.m.
$5
From Bismarck, head West on I-94 toward Billings. In 112.0 miles, take exit 42 onto US-85 toward Belfield. In 0.2 miles, turn left onto US-85. In 57.0 miles, turn left onto 3rd Street NE. In 0.6 miles, turn right onto East Divide Street. In 700 feet, your destination will be on your right.

McKenzie County Pioneer Museum (historical)
Main Street S, Watford City, North Dakota 58854
(701)444-2990
Monday–Saturday 10:00 a.m.–5:00 p.m.
Free
From Bismarck, head west on I-94 toward Billings. In 112.0 miles, take exit 42 onto US-85 toward Belfield. In 0.2 miles, turn right onto US-85. In 63.0 miles, take a slight right turn onto ND-23. In 0.6 miles, turn left onto Bus US-85. In 2.1 miles, continue onto Main Street South. In 350 feet, you will arrive at your destination.

Three Affiliated Tribes Museum (archaeological)

404 Frontage Road, New Town, North Dakota 58763

(701)627-4477

Monday–Friday 10:00 a.m.–4:00 p.m.

Donation

From Bismarck, head west on I-94 toward Billings. In 7.9 miles, take exit 147 onto ND-25 toward Center Stanton. In 0.2 miles, turn right onto ND-25. In 19.0 miles, turn right onto 28th Avenue SW. In 11.0 miles, turn right onto SH-200 Alt. In 4.4 miles, turn left onto US-83 North. In 51.0 miles, turn left onto 247th Avenue SE. In 56.0 miles, your destination will be on your right.

Menoken Indian Village (archaeological)

Menoken, North Dakota 58558 (701)328-2666

Donations

Daily

From Bismarck, head east on I-94 toward Fargo. In 11.0 miles, take exit 170 toward Menoken. In 0.2 miles, turn left onto 158th Street NE. In 0.2 miles, turn right onto 30th Avenue NE. In 1.0 mile, turn left onto 171st Street NE. In 0.2 miles, prepare to park your vehicle near 171st Street NE. Your destination will be on your right.

Double Ditch Indian Village (archaeological; hiking required)

ND-1804, Bismarck, North Dakota 58503

Daily

Free

From Fargo, head west on I-94 toward Bismarck. In 189.0 miles, take exit onto Bismarck Expressway. In 0.2 miles, turn right onto Centennial Road. In 6.3 miles, at the roundabout, take the second exit onto ND-1804. In 6.6 miles, take a slight left turn onto Double Ditch Loop. In 0.4 miles, prepare to park your vehicle, your destination will be on your right.

Knife River Indian Village (archaeological)

564 CR-37, Stanton, North Dakota 58571

(701)745-3309

Daily

Free

From Bismarck, head west I-94 toward Billings. In 7.9 miles, take exit 147 onto ND-25 toward Center Stanton. In 0.2 miles, turn right onto ND-25. In 29.0 miles, turn right onto Center Avenue South. In 9.3 miles, turn left onto State Highway 200 Alt. In 6.2 miles, turn right onto ND-31. In 1.9 miles, continue onto CR-37. In 0.5 miles, turn right. Your destination will be on your left.

Turtle Mountain Chippewa Heritage Center (archaeological)
3959 Skydancer Way NE, Belcourt, North Dakota 58316
(701)244-5530
Monday–Friday 8:00 a.m.–4:30 p.m.
Donation
From Bismarck, head south on US-83 toward Fargo. In 23.0 miles, take exit 182 onto US-83 South. In 0.3 miles, turn left onto 314th Street. In 900 feet, continue onto 314th Street. In 73.0 miles, continue onto County Road 11. In 10.0 miles, turn right onto 42nd Street NE. In 14.0 miles, turn left onto ND-3. In 25.0 miles, turn left onto 1st Street NW. In 31.0 miles, turn right onto US-281. In 9.6 miles, turn left onto Skydancer Way. In 700 feet, turn right. In 0.3 miles, you will arrive at your destination.

South Dakota

Grand River Museum (obscure)

114 Tenth Street W, Lemmon, South Dakota 57638

(605)374-3911

May–September Monday–Saturday 9:00 a.m.–5:30 p.m.; Sunday 12:00 p.m.–5:00 p.m.

Donation

From Rapid City, head west on I-90 toward Gillette. In 21.0 miles, take exit 37 onto Pleasant Valley Road. In 0.2 miles, turn right onto Pleasant Valley Road. In 0.9 miles, turn left onto Fort Meade Way. In 5.1 miles, turn left onto SD-34. In 0.3 miles, turn right onto SD-79. In 22.0 miles, turn right onto 8th Street. In 72.0 miles, turn left onto SD-73. In 64.0 miles, turn right onto 10th Street West. In 0.7 miles, turn right. In 40 feet, turn left. Your destination will be on your right.

Pioneer Auto Show Museum (obscure)

503 E 5th Street, Murdo, South Dakota 57559

(605)669-2691

8:30 a.m.–8:30 p.m.

$10

From Rapid City, head east on I-90 toward Sioux Falls. In 135.0 miles, take exit 192 onto US-83 toward Murdo. In 0.2 miles, turn left onto US-83 toward Murdo. In 800 feet, continue onto I-90 BL. In 800 feet, turn left into the parking lot. In 250 feet, your destination will be on your left.

Storybook Island Fun Center (obscure)

1301 Sheridan Lake Road, Rapid City, South Dakota 57702

(605)342-6357

Memorial Day–Labor Day 9:00 a.m.–7:00 p.m.

Free

From Spearfish, head east on I-90. In 43.0 miles, take exit 55 onto Deadwood Avenue. In 0.2 miles, keep right onto Deadwood Avenue. In 2.3 miles, turn right onto West Chicago Street. In 800 feet, turn left onto Sheffer Street. In 0.2 miles, turn right onto West Main Street. In 700 feet, turn left onto Sheridan Lake Road. In 0.6 miles, turn right. Your destination will be on your left.

The Ranch Store/Six Ton Prairie Dog Statue (obscure)

21190 SD-240, Long Valley, South Dakota 57567

(605)433-5477

24-7 (prairie dog) May–October 8:00 a.m.–6:00 p.m. (store)

Free

From Rapid City. head east on I-90 toward Sioux Falls. In 74.0 miles, take exit 131 onto SD-240 toward Interior. In 0.3 miles, turn right onto SD-240. In 1.2 miles, your destination will be on your right.

Dinosaur Statue Park (obscure)

940 Skyline Drive, Rapid City, South Dakota 57701

(605)394-4175

Monday–Friday 8:00 a.m.–5:00 p.m.

Free

From Spearfish, head east on I-90. In 45.0 miles, take exit 57 onto US-16 West toward downtown. In 1.5 miles, continue onto West Boulevard. In 0.4 miles, turn right onto Quincy Street. In 1.0 mile, your destination will be on your right.

John Lopez Sculpture Gallery (obscure)

304 Main Avenue, Lemmon, South Dakota 57638

(605) 209-0954

Monday–Saturday 10:00 a.m.–3:00 p.m.

Free

From Rapid City, head east on I-90. In 18.0 miles, take exit 78 onto 61st Avenue. In 0.2 miles, turn left onto 161st Avenue. In 32.0 miles, turn right onto SD-34. In 40.0 miles, turn left onto SD-73. In 28.0 miles, turn left onto West First Street. In 3.1 miles, turn right on SD-73. In 64.0 miles, turn right onto 10th Street West. In 0.8 miles, turn left onto Main Avenue. In 0.5 miles, your destination will be on your right.

Wall Drug Store (obscure)

510 Main Street, Wall, South Dakota

(605)279-2175

Monday–Saturday 8:00 a.m.–5:30 p.m.; Sunday 8:00 a.m.–4:30 p.m.

Free

From Rapid City, head east on I-90 toward Sioux Falls. In 52.0 miles, take exit 109 toward I-90 BL. In 0.3 miles, turn left onto SD-240 toward I-90 BL. In 0.2 miles, stay left onto SD-240. In 0.7 miles, turn right onto Main Street. In 450 feet, turn left onto 5th Avenue. Your destination will be on your right.

Skeleton Man/Skeleton Dinosaur (obscure; can be seen from highway; do not stop on highway)

I-90 Belvidere, South Dakota 57521

24-7

Free

From Rapid City, head east on I-90. In 115.0 miles, take exit 172 onto Stamford Road. In 0.2 miles, turn left onto Stamford Road. Turn left to merge onto I-90. In 1.6 miles, prepare to park your vehicle.

Termesphere Art Gallery (obscure)

1920 Christensen Drive, Spearfish, South Dakota 57783

(605)642-4805

9:00 a.m.–5:00 p.m.

Free to look

From Rapid City, head west on I-90 toward Gillette. In 43.0 miles, take exit 14 toward I-90 BL. In 800 feet, keep left toward Spearfish Canyon Byway. In 600 feet, turn left onto North 27th Street. In 500 feet, turn right onto East Colorado Boulevard. In 0.5 miles, turn left onto Christensen Drive. In 1.7 miles, your destination will be on your left.

The Corn Palace (obscure)

604 N Main Street, Mitchell, South Dakota 57301

(605)995-8430

8:00 a.m.–9:00 p.m.

Free

From Sioux Falls, head west on I-90 toward Rapid City. In 64.0 miles, take exit 332 onto I-90 BL South toward Mitchell. In 0.2 miles, turn right onto South Burr Street. In 1.2 miles, turn left onto East 1st Avenue. In 0.3 miles, turn right onto North Main Street. In 0.4 miles, your destination will be on your right.

Chapel in the Hills (obscure)

(605)342-8281

3788 Chapel Lane, Rapid City, South Dakota 57702

8:00 a.m.–8:00 p.m.

Free to Look

From Spearfish, head east on I-90. In 43.0 miles, take exit 55 onto Deadwood Avenue. In 0.2 miles, keep right onto Deadwood Avenue. In 2.3 miles, turn left onto West Chicago Street. In 800 feet, turn left onto Shaffer Street. In 0.2 miles, turn right onto West Main Street. In 700 feet, turn left onto Sheridan Lake Road. In 0.8 miles, turn right onto Jackson Boulevard. In 1.8 miles, turn left onto Chapel Lane. In 0.3 miles, keep left onto Chapel Lane. In 0.7 miles, turn left into the parking lot. In 300 feet, your destination will be on your right.

Evans Plunge Indoor Hot Springs (obscure)

1145 N River Street, Hot Springs, South Dakota 57747
(605)745-5165
Monday–Friday 6:00 a.m.–10:00 a.m.; 11:00 a.m.–4:00 p.m.
Saturday–Sunday 10:00 a.m.–2:00 p.m.; 3:00 p.m.–7:00 p.m.
$12
From Rapid City, head west on US-16. In 23.0 miles, turn right onto Mount Rushmore Road. In 0.5 miles, turn left onto Centennial Drive. In 30.0 miles, turn right onto North River Street. In 400 feet, your destination will be on your right.

Children's Museum of South Dakota (obscure)

521 Fourth Street, Brookings, South Dakota 57006 (605)692-6700
Tuesday–Saturday 10:00 a.m.–5:00 p.m.
Free
From Sioux Falls, head north on I-29 toward Brookings. In 52.0 miles, take exit 132 onto US-14 toward Brookings. In 0.3 miles, turn left onto 6th Street. In 1.6 miles, turn left onto Medary Avenue. In 900 feet, turn right onto 4th Street. In 0.4 miles, your destination will be on your right.

Storybookland Augmented Statue Park (obscure)

2310 24th Avenue, NW, Aberdeen, South Dakota 57401
(605)626-7015
10:00 a.m.–9:00 p.m.
$2.25
From Sioux Falls, head north on I-29 toward Brookings. In 126.0 miles, take exit 207 onto US-12 toward Aberdeen. In 0.2 miles, turn left onto US-12 toward Aberdeen. In 70.0 miles, turn right onto 391st Avenue South. In 3.0 miles, turn left onto 130th Street NE. In 5.0 miles, turn left onto US-281 South. In 0.8 miles, turn right onto Sertoma Parkway. You have arrived at your destination.

Cosmos Mystery Area (obscure)

24040 Cosmos Road, Rapid City, South Dakota 57702
(605)343-9802

9:00 a.m.–5:00 p.m.

$11(Mystery House tour); $8 (Geode Mine)

From Spearfish, head east on I-90. In 45.0 miles, take exit 57 onto US-16 West toward Mount Rushmore. In 1.5 miles, turn left onto Omaha Street. In 0.2 miles, turn right onto Mount Rushmore Road. In 17.0 miles, turn left onto Cosmos Road. In 0.6 miles, turn left. In 40 feet, your destination will be on your left.

Petrified Wood Park and Museum (obscure)

500 Main Avenue, Lemmon, South Dakota 57638

(605)374-3964

March 1–May 15 Friday, Saturday, Sunday 10:00 a.m.–5:00 p.m.

May 16–September 15 daily 10:00 a.m.–4:00 p.m.

Donations

From Spearfish, head west on I-90 toward Gillete. In 1.8 miles, take exit 10 onto US-85 North toward Belle Fourche. In 0.3 miles, turn right US-85 North toward Center of the Nation. In 11.0 miles, continue onto Fifth Avenue. In 32.0 miles, turn right onto SD-168. In 6.9 miles, turn left onto SD-79. In 49.0 miles, turn right onto SD-20. In 45.0 miles, turn left onto SD-73. In 28.0 miles, turn right onto Tenth Street West. In 0.8 miles, turn left onto Main Avenue. In 0.3 miles, your destination will be on your right.

Porter Sculpture Park (obscure)

25700 451st Avenue, Montrose, South Dakota 57048

(605)204-0370

7:00 a.m.–8:30 p.m.

$10

From Sioux Falls, head north on I-29 toward Brookings. In 3.1 miles, take exit 84B to merge onto I-90 West toward Rapid City. In 22.0 miles, take exit 374 toward Montrose. In 0.3 miles, turn left onto 451st Avenue. In 0.6 miles, turn left onto 257th Street. In 1.1 miles, prepare to park your vehicle near 257th Street.

Devils Gulch (nature; hiking required)
(605)594-6721
Center Avenue, Garretson, South Dakota 57030
8:00 a.m.–8:00 p.m.
Free
From Sioux Falls, head north on I-229. In 3.9 miles, take exit 10A to merge onto I-90 East. In 5.9 miles, take exit 406 onto SD-11 toward Corson. In 0.2 miles, turn left onto North Splitrock Boulevard. In 10.0 miles, turn right onto 5th Street. In 0.4 miles, turn left onto 5th Street. In 400 feet, turn left onto Devils Gulch Park Road. In 0.4 miles, take a slight right turn onto Center Avenue. You have arrived at your destination.

Black Hills Caverns (nature)
2600 Cavern Road, Rapid City, South Dakota 57702
(605)343-0542
June–August 9:00 a.m.–6:00 p.m.; May–September 9:00 a.m.–5:00 p.m. (September only weekends; closed during winter)
$13.95+
From Spearfish, head east on I-90. In 43.0 miles, take exit 55 onto Deadwood Avenue. In 0.2 miles, keep right onto Deadwood Avenue. In 2.2 miles, turn left onto West Omaha Street. In 0.3 miles, turn right onto Mountain View Road. In 0.5 miles, turn right onto Jackson Boulevard. In 6.0 miles, turn right onto Cavern Road. In 0.4 miles, turn left. You have arrived at your destination.

Black Elk Peak (nature; hiking required)

Keystone, South Dakota 57751

24-7

Free

From Rapid City, head west on US-16. In 18.0 miles, keep right onto US-16 West. In 13.0 miles, turn left onto SD-87. In 5.8 miles, turn left onto SD-87. In 0.9 miles, turn left. In 200 feet, prepare to park your vehicle near Little Devil's Tower, head left onto Little Devil's Tower. In 90 feet, take a sharp right turn onto Little Devil's Tower. In 2.7 miles, take a right turn onto Harney 9 south. In 0.3 miles, take a left onto Harney 9 south. In 0.2 miles, your destination will be on your left.

Falls Park (nature)

131 E Falls Park Drive, Sioux Falls, South Dakota 57104

(605)367-7430

5:00 a.m.–12:00 a.m.

$20

From Brookings, head south on I-29 toward Sioux Falls. In 51.0 miles, take exit 81 onto Maple Street. In 0.6 miles, turn left onto West Maple Street. In 2.9 miles, turn right onto East Walnut Street. In 150 feet, turn right onto North 1st Avenue. In 0.5 miles, turn left. Your destination will be on your right.

Rushmore Cave (nature)

13622 Highway 40, Keystone, South Dakota 57751

(605)255-4384

Sunday–Thursday 9:00 a.m.–5:00 p.m.

$11+

From Rapid City, head west on US-16. In 12.0 miles, keep left. In 0.4 miles, turn left onto South Rockerville Road. In 5.7 miles, turn left onto SD-40. In 3.3 miles, turn left onto Rushmore Cave Roadl. In 900 feet, your destination will be on your right.

Roughlock Falls Trail (nature; hiking required)

10619 Roughlock Falls Road, Lead, South Dakota 57754

(605)584-3896

24-7

Free

From Rapid City, head west on I-90 toward Gillette. In 43.0 miles, take exit 14 toward I-90 BL. In 800 feet, keep left toward Spearfish Canyon Bypass. In 600 feet, turn left onto North 27th Street. In 500 feet, turn right onto East Colorado Boulevard. In 1.6 miles, turn left onto Spearfish

Canyon Road. In 13.0 miles, turn right onto Roughlock Falls Road. In 300 feet, turn left. You have arrived at your destination.

Custer State Park (nature)
13329 US Highway 16A, Custer, South Dakota 57730
(605)255-4515
24-7
$20
From Rapid City, head west on US-16. In 7.1 miles, turn left onto Neck Yoke Road. In 0.4 miles, turn left onto Spring Creek Road. In 4.8 miles, turn right onto SD-79. In 9.2 miles, take a slight right turn onto SD-36. In 9.2 miles, take a slight right turn. You have arrived at your destination.

Badlands State Park (nature)
(605)433-5361
25216 Ben Reifel Road, Interior, South Dakota 57750
24-7
$30
From Rapid City, take I-90 east. In 74.0 miles, take exit 131 onto SD-240 toward Interior. In 0.3 miles, turn right onto SD-240. In 3.5 miles, continue onto SD-240 West. In 8.1 miles, turn left onto Ben Reifel Road. In 150 feet, turn left. Your destination will be on your right.

Wind Cave National Park (nature)
26611 US-385 Hot Springs, South Dakota 57747
(605) 745-4600
8:00 a.m.–4:30 p.m.
$12
From Rapid City, head west on US-16. In 18.0 miles, keep right onto US-16 West. In 23.0 miles, turn right onto Mount Rushmore Road. In 0.5 miles, turn left onto Centennial Drive. In 21.0 miles, turn right. In 0.5 miles, keep left. In 900 feet, your destination will be on your right.

Hugh Glass Memorial (historical)
Hugh Glass Road, Lemmon, South Dakota 57638
24-7
Free
From Rapid City, head west on I-90 toward Gillette. In 21.0 miles, take exit 1A to merge onto Pleasant Valley Road. In 0.2 miles, turn right onto Pleasant Valley Road. In 0.9 miles, turn left onto Fort Meade Way. In 5.1 miles, turn left onto SD-34. In 0.3 miles, turn right onto SD-79. In 22.0 miles, turn right onto 8th Street. In 72 miles, turn left onto SD-73. In 52.0 miles, turn left onto Hugh Glass Road. In 3.9 miles, your destination will be on your right.

Mount Rushmore (historical)
13000 SD Highway 244, Keystone, South Dakota 57751
(605)574-2523
5:00 a.m.–11:00 p.m.
Free
From Rapid City, head west on US-16. In 18.0 miles, keep left onto US-16 West. In 3.8 miles, continue onto SD-244. In 1.5 miles, take a slight right turn. In 300 feet, your destination will be on your left.

South Dakota State Railroad Museum/1880's Train (historical)
222 Railroad Avenue, Hill City, South Dakota 57745
(605)574-2222
1800train.com (Check website for train schedule.)
$27
From Rapid City, head west on US-16. In 17.0 miles, keep right onto US-16 West. In 9.1 miles, turn left onto Railroad Avenue. In 700 feet, turn left. Your destination will be on your right.

Jewel Cave Monument (historical)
11149 US Highway 16, Custer, South Dakota
(605)673-8300
Thursday–Sunday 8:30 a.m.–4:30 p.m.
$8
From Rapid City, head west on US-16. In 18.0 miles, keep right onto US-16 West. In 23.0 miles, turn right onto Mount Rushmore Road. In 12.0 miles, turn left. In 0.6 miles, turn right. In 0.2 miles, your destination will be on your left.

Big Thunder Gold Mine (historical)
(605)666-4847
604 Blair Street, Keystone, South Dakota 57751
8:00 a.m.–8:00 p.m.
$11.95
From Rapid City, head west on US-16 west. In 3.4 miles, turn left onto Mt Rushmore Road. In 13.0 miles, keep left. In 2.7 miles, turn left onto Reed Street. In 0.4 miles, turn right onto Blair Street. In 150 feet, turn left onto Blair Street. In 250 feet, your destination will be on your right.

Buffalo Ridge 1880 Cowboy Town (historical)

46614 West SD-38, Buffalo Ridge, South Dakota 57107

(605)528-3931

9:00 a.m.–7:00 p.m.

$8

From Sioux Falls, head north on I-29. In 3.4 miles, take exit 83 toward airport. In 0.3 miles, turn left onto SD-38. In 6.0 miles, your destination will be on your right.

Dignity of Earth and Sky (historical; located at the information center)

I-90 Mile Marker 264, Chamberlain, South Dakota 57325

(605) 734-4562

24-7

Free

From Sioux Falls, head west on I-90 toward Rapid City. In 132.0 miles, take a slight right turn. In 1.2 miles, prepare to park your vehicle. In 150 feet, your destination will be on your right.

America's Founding Fathers Exhibit (historical)

9815 S. US Highway 16, Rapid City, South Dakota (605)877-6043

9:00 a.m.–4:00 p.m.

$10

From Spearfish, head east on I-90. In 45.0 miles, take exit 57 onto US-16 West toward downtown. In 1.5 miles, turn left onto Omaha Street. In 0.2 miles, turn right onto Mount Rushmore Road. In 7.6 miles, turn right. In 250 feet, you will arrive at your destination.

Graves of Wild Bill and Calamity Jane (historical)

(605)722-0837

1 Mount Moriah Drive, Deadwood, South Dakota 57732

8:00 a.m.–6:00 p.m.

Free

From Spearfish, head south on US-85. In 5.5 miles, take exit 17 onto US-85 South toward Deadwood. In 0.3 miles, turn right onto US-85 South. In 7.4 miles, turn right onto Main Street. In 1.1 miles, turn left onto Lee Street. In 200 feet, turn right onto Sherman Street. In 0.3 miles, turn left onto Cemetery Street. In 100 feet, turn right onto Van Buren Avenue. In 150 feet, turn left onto Lincoln Avenue. In 450 feet, turn left onto Jackson Street. In 800 feet, turn right onto Mount Moriah Drive. In 150 feet, your destination will be on your left.

Broken Boot Gold Mine (historical)

1200 Pioneer Way, Deadwood, South Dakota 57732

(605)578-9997

June 1–Labor Day 8:00 a.m.–6:00 p.m.

$8

From Rapid City, head east on I-90 toward Gillette. In 28.0 miles, take exit 30 onto Lazelle Street toward Deadwood. In 800 feet, turn left onto Lazelle Street. In 600 feet, continue onto Lazelle Street. In 13.0 miles, your destination will be on your right.

Museum of Geology (historical)
501 East Saint Joseph Street, Rapid City, South Dakota 57701
(605)394-2467
Monday–Saturday 9:00 a.m.–6:00 p.m.
Free
From Spearfish, head east on I-90. In 45.0 miles, take exit 57 onto US-16 West toward down-town. In 1.5 miles, turn left onto Omaha Street. In 0.2 miles, continue onto Omaha Street. In 0.8 miles, turn right onto East Boulevard. In 0.2 miles, turn left onto East Saint Joseph Street. In 0.6 miles, turn right onto University Loop. In 0.2 miles, turn right. In 800 feet, your destination will be on your right.

Death Chair of Wild Bill/Original Saloon No. 10 (historical)
657 Main Street, Deadwood, South Dakota 57732 (800)952-9398
9:00 a.m.–1:30 a.m.
Free to look

From Spearfish, head south on US-85. In 5.5 miles, take exit 17 onto US-85 South toward Deadwood. In 0.3 miles, turn right onto US-85 South. In 7.4 miles, turn right onto Main Street. In 1.1 miles, turn right onto Wall Street. In 200 feet, turn left onto Main Street. In 350 feet, your destination will be on your left.

Hotel Alex Johnson (historical)
523 6th Street, Rapid City, South Dakota 57701
(605)342-1210
24-7
Free to look
From Spearfish, head east on I-90. In 45.0 miles, take exit 57 onto US-16 West toward downtown. In 1.5 miles, turn left onto Omaha Street. In 0.2 miles, continue onto Omaha Street. In 0.2 miles, turn right onto 6th Street. In 0.2 miles, your destination will be on your right.

Chief Crazy Horse Memorial (historical)
12151 Avenue of the Chiefs, Crazy Horse, South Dakota 57730
(605)673-4681
9:00 a.m.–5:00 p.m.
$11 single entry; $20 for vehicle

From Rapid City, head west on US-16. In 18.0 miles, keep right onto US-16 West. In 19.0 miles, turn left onto Avenue of the Chiefs. In 0.7 miles, turn left into the parking lot. You have arrived at your destination.

St. Peter's Rock Grotto (historical)
3rd Street, Farmer, South Dakota 57311
24-7
Free
From Sioux Falls, head north on I-29 toward Brookings. In 3.1 miles, take exit 84B to merge onto I-90 West toward Rapid City. In 46.0 miles, take exit 350 onto SD-25 toward Farmer. In 0.3 miles, turn right onto SD-25 toward Farmer. In 2.4 miles, turn left onto SD-38. In 1.0 mile, turn right onto 426th Avenue. In 1.7 miles, turn left onto 3rd Street. In 200 feet, your destination will be on your left.

Mammoth Site (historical)
1800 US 18 Bypass, Hot Springs, South Dakota 57747
(605)745-6017
Monday–Saturday 9:00 a.m.–3:30 p.m.; Sunday 11:00 a.m.–3:30 p.m.
$10
From Rapid City, head west on US-16. In 7.1 miles, turn left onto Neck Yoke Road. In 0.4 miles, turn left onto Spring Creek Road. In 4.8 miles, turn right onto SD-79. In 42.0 miles, turn right

onto Fall River Road. In 4.1 miles, turn left onto Indianapolis Avenue. In 1.1 miles, your destination will be on your right.

Spirit Mound Historic Prairie (archeological)
31148 SD-19, Vermillion, South Dakota 57069
(605)987-2263
6:00 a.m.–11:00 p.m.
Free
From Sioux Falls, head south on I-29. In 36.0 miles, take exit 38 toward Volin. In 0.3 miles, turn right onto 306th Street. In 8.5 miles, turn left onto SD-19. In 6.2 miles, turn right, your destination will be on your right.

Tatanka: Story of the Bison (archaeological)
100 Tatanka Drive, Deadwood, South Dakota 57732
(605)584-5678
Friday–Sunday 10:00 a.m.–4:00 p.m.
$20
From Rapid City, head west on I-90 toward Gillette. In 28.0 miles, take exit 30 onto Lazelle Street toward Deadwood. In 800 feet, turn left onto Lazelle Street. In 600 feet, continue onto Lazelle Street. In 11.0 miles, turn right onto US-85. In 0.9 miles, your destination will be on your right.

About the Author

Madison Gabrielle is a free-spirited, adventure-seeking, modern-day nomad. She is one of those special souls born with deep wanderlust. Madison was born in South Louisiana. Her early years were spent traveling to different cities for gymnastics. At twenty-two, she took off for the High Rockies—just because she had never seen snow.

Madison has lived in, and visited, several other states since leaving Louisiana. While living in California, her dear friend passed away while adventuring in Canada with his dog. Madison drove to the Canadian border to rescue her friend's faithful companion, Spud. Along the way, she discovered that Spud needed to be quarantined for an extended period of time. During that waiting period, Madison explored the surrounding states, discovering a treasure trove of eccentric and breathtaking roadside attractions. Since then, she's covered even more ground, exploring, documenting, and, yes, looking for even more hidden treasures.

It is her heartfelt hope that her books inspire you to explore this world, its beauty, and its oddities. She wants you to immerse yourself in the land that is yours. You may even stumble upon hidden gems yet to be discovered. Turn a simple road trip into an unforgettable journey. Expand your world with her off-the-beaten-path expeditions. Get out there!